DO EVERY THING WRONG!

PUBLISHED BY WE HEARD YOU LIKE BOOKS
A Division of U2603 LLC
5419 Hollywood Blvd, Ste C-231 Los Angeles CA 90027

http://weheardyoulikebooks.com/

ISBN: 978-0-692-03998-4

Decemember 2018

10 9 8 7 6 5 4 3 2 1

DO EVERY THING WRONG!

JARETT KOBEK

XXXTENTACION AGAINST THE WORLD

WE HEARD YOU LIKE BOOKS
2018

CHAPTER 1

MAKE AMERICA GAPE AGAIN

You know how this story ends.

Everyone does.

With a bullet in the neck.

*

About a month after he died, I decided that I should read his tweets.

All of them.

From beginning until end.

After three years of fucking with his music, and two years of being irritated by his media coverage, it occurred to me that his Twitter might give some insight into who he was and, like The Bat-Man, how he came to be.

·

XXXTentacion's account has over 53,000 tweets.

No one can scroll that far back, as it'll crash a browser and destroy a mind.

And the Twitter API only allows access to any account's last 3,200 tweets.

·

I found software on GitHub that would search, day by day, through XXXTentacion's tweets and capture them into a file readable by Microsoft Excel.

But I had no idea how to run the software.

I asked a friend for help.

·

We decided not to capture the retweets.

Even I have limits.

She sent me the results, which were about four megabytes in size.

It contained 26,654 tweets.

http://weheardyoulikebooks.com/xxx.xlsx.

·

The tweets date from 13 August 2012 AD, when his account was @fuckjahseh and the idea of XXXTentacion didn't exist, until 28 June 2018 AD, when his account was @xxxtentacion and his management tweeted on behalf of his grieving mother.

25,882 of the tweets predate his arrest on 14 July 2016 AD for, allegedly, stabbing and robbing his former manager.

771 are after.

*

When the criminal justice system began intersecting with his media coverage, he started deleting tweets.

But most of the deletions were recent.

The older tweets remain unchanged, unaffected.

*

14 July 2016 AD begins the last twenty-three months of his life.

This period contains almost every incident of note.

The further arrests, the jail time, the disastrous tours, the model's suicide, the worldly success, the album releases, the rise to ultimate and crushing fame.

Less than two years.

An insane way to live.

*

Those twenty-three months also coincide with almost nonstop media coverage.

The vast majority of this coverage was negative in its tone but contained a factual core.

If we combine his tweets with this manufactured morality, we can achieve a portrait of his life from the age of fourteen.

But we know almost nothing about what happened before 13 August 2012 AD.

*

On 23 January 1998 AD, he is born.

They call him Jahseh Dwayne Ricardo Onfroy.

His infant body emerges from the womb into Florida.

Broward County.

The heart of Weird Florida.

The Florida Man meme and the perpetual electoral recount.

It's where Jahseh Onfroy will live his whole life.

And where he will die.

*

His mother is young and named Cleopatra.

She's 18.

His father is named Dwayne Ricardo Onfroy.

He's 24 years old.

He's a Rasta.

*

In interviews before his death, XXXTentacion talked about the difficulties of his early childhood.

He painted a portrait of the requisite traumatic upbringing—neglect, shuffled from house to house, time in a group home, getting kicked out of schools, the beatings both received and administered, living with a grandmother who herself hasn't broken 35 years of age when he was born, the difficulty and occasional violence of a single mother bringing new men into the home.

*

His father was absent, a casualty of the United States government and its multi-decade War on Drugs, which was, and is, a systemic conspiracy to ruin the lives of several generations of Black men.

*

Dwayne Onfroy goes down in a sting.

This is in Phoenix, Arizona.

This is in 2008 AD.

He pleads out to two of four charges.

Money laundering and attempting to sell hundreds of pounds of weed.

His sentence is 108 months in prison.

Much later, on petition, Obama-era changes in sentencing laws reduce his stint by nearly a year.

*

XXXTentacion's father is arrested on 19 March 2008 AD.

He remains in custody until November 2015 AD.

He goes in when his son is ten years old.

He comes out when his son is seventeen and on the cusp of worldwide fame.

*

On 6 March 2014 AD, XXXTentacion tweets: "so fucking happy , my dad called me , asked me to rap for all his homies on the cell block , and them niggas all freaked out"

And follows it up with: "nigga told me he was proud of me"

*

As mentioned: his father's money laundering charge, and the mandatory drug sentencing, are the products of a governmental conspiracy.

Both derived from legislation signed into law by President Ronald Wilson Reagan.

Who loved anti-drug rhetoric and policy.

His wife came up with JUST SAY NO.

Reagan and his wife spent the 1980s telling kids to not do drugs.

*

At the very same time that the televised President lectured a generation about the evils of drugs, he was overriding the will of Congress.

He was funding anti-Communist forces in Nicaragua.

This was actively against the law.

By any conceivable measure, he was a criminal.

And the worst of it?

Reagan, and his subordinates, knew that the people fighting against Nicaraguan communism were also dealing drugs.

They were moving cocaine into these United States, a country with an insatiable appetite for blotting out its own horrors through sensorium pleasures.

And Reagan and his subordinates looked the other way.

They created the crack epidemic.

Which ruined the lives of countless of Black people.

Which created the social situations that produced hysterical legislation.

Which put XXXTentacion's father in a federal prison.

*

This isn't speculation.

Or conspiracy theory.

This is a matter of public record.

The President was a criminal.

His subordinates were criminals.

They operated at a level of criminality rare in American life.

At best, they turned a blind eye to the creation of a drug epidemic.

Some of these Presidential aides were convicted for their crimes.

None of them served a day in prison.

One of them, who, as the head of the CIA, had supported the money laundering and drug dealing of Manuel Noriega, became the President after Reagan.

His name was George Bush.

The first George Bush.

And as President, he went to war against Manuel Noriega.

For the drug dealing.

And he threw Noriega's ass into Federal Prison.

In Florida.

*

And Dwayne Onfroy got eight years in pokey for trying to sell some weed to an undercover fed.

And his son lived without a father.

*

This, then, is the story of XXXTentacion's early life.

It isn't the litany of suffering that is mandatory in every biography.

It's the story of how systemic influences in a society shape and create the contours of an individual.

And it starts with the governmental conspiracy to put several generations of Black men into prison.

And the pathology that this conspiracy has wreaked on the children of those Black men.

The constructed behaviors.

And the hypocrisy of a society that tolerates unspeakable crimes from its highest elected officials but brooks no forgiveness for the sins of its poor.

It's a story about the kid who gets a call from his father and raps for jailbirds.

And it's a story about someone breaking out.

And crashing back in.

CHAPTER 2

U LIKE IT REAL

When Jahseh Onfroy starts his Twitter account on 13 August 2012 AD, he doesn't know it, but he's creating a new self.

In this moment, on his iPhone, he's just another lost boy in Florida.

As far as we know, he's never recorded a single bar.

He hasn't thought up the name XXXTentacion.

He's fourteen.

*

He uses Twitter as an unfiltered confessional.

It's more than just the blasé blasé affectation of a teenager induced to transform every passing thought into monetizable content for his Silicon Valley overlords.

Reading the tweets, you come to the realization that this is a person of unusual honesty.

*

He tweets about shit that anyone with any good sense wouldn't put on the Internet.

A ton of law-breaking, much while under house arrest or on probation.

It never seemed to bite him on the ass, which tells you about his pre-fame importance in the hierarchy of criminal justice.

They didn't even monitor his social media.

*

There's a thing that happens, over and over again.

He'll get into an argument on Twitter and then demand the address of the person with whom he's arguing.

Sometimes, people are stupid enough to give him the address.

Or an enemy rats them out.

This is followed by a succession of tweets in which XXXTentacion is on his way to this someone's house, is outside someone's house, and tweeting after he's fought the person.

There's also a lot of tweets about his broken hands.

*

His sex drive and sex life are discussed in endless detail.

That dude fucked a lot.

And while he was young, too.

He preferred Latinas.

One relationship dominates the early years, inspiring both music and tattoos.

*

When he's still @fuckjahseh, XXXTentacion communicates with people who aren't wired into the world of music.

They're kids he goes to high school with, girls that he's fucking, people he knows from around.

The vast majority of these people deleted their accounts.

The remaining conversations are spectral, one-sided, fragmented, Jahseh only.

*

By the time the other kids from Broward County decide that they should delete their accounts, @fuckjahseh has become @XXXTentacion.

And he's well on his way to being famous.

And he'd linked that fame to a Twitter account he started when he was fourteen years old.

*

The way that you use a tool, initially, is the basis of how you always use that tool.

*

All the other kids from Broward County had the luxury of growing up.

Of changing.

But he was locked into the persona that he'd created when was fourteen, and that persona became the center of his whole public self.

*

He wasn't kidding about his many statements regarding mental illness.

The tweets make it obvious that something was wrong.

And this isn't just because social media is indistinguishable from mental illness.

*

Think about the craziest people in American public life.

You know who I mean.

They're also the most famous.

What is the commonality between them?

Twitter.

*

There's an edge to his many calls for his own death, and their frequency, and his own professions of emptiness, and his ability to turn from love to hate on a dime.

You can go on Twitter at any moment of the day and find teenagers tweeting about how they want to die.

But I defy you to find another who's tweeting their address and asking people to come shoot them in the head.

*

In the files of Broward County, there's a traffic citation that XXXTentacion received on 29 August 2015 AD.

He was with a young woman.

They were on the side of a road.

They were having an argument.

Whatever happened, it upset XXXTentacion.

He jumped into the road and ran into a car that was traveling at 30 miles per hour.

The police report says that he hit the car with enough force to cause significant damage.

He was that kind of crazy.

*

There are two tweets from that night.

The first reads: "I hate hospitals."

The second reads: "I should be dead."

*

Here are a quick succession of tweets issued across seventy minutes on 5 June 2015 AD:

"I wanna die again."

"I need to cum."

"I'm going to."

"I give up on you."

"If they wont chase you to the ends of the earth, they don't love you."

"if you let the person you love walk away from you, you're either weak as fuck, or don't love them."

"kill me , please."

"goodbye."

*

But this is the day-to-day.

Regular teenager shit: violence, drugs, sex, difficulties with authority, another Black kid ensnared in the world of criminal justice.

*

Seven months after he opens his Twitter account, on 14 May 2013 AD, he is arrested.

He's fifteen years old.

This arrest, apparently his first, is the most important thing that will happen in his short life.

*

It goes down while he's hitting licks.

He's a juvenile, so the full record is sealed.

It's difficult to find out what happened.

We only know what he told interviewers.

And we only know its consequences.

CHAPTER 3

BARELY BRE4THING BUT STILL SCREAMING

Fast forward to April 2016 AD.

XXXTentacion goes to Los Angeles.

He does a long interview with the *No Jumper* podcast.

For the first time, he offers up the details of his life in an easily consumable fashion.

*

Prior to this, his story is scattered piecemeal across social media platforms.

And the people who write about music are lazy.

They aren't going to piece the story together.

By appearing on the podcast, he's doing a favor to the individuals who end up as his greatest adversaries in public life.

He's giving them the backbone of their indignation.

And, alas, this is the interview in which he talks about juvenile detention.

*

No Jumper is a run out of a BMX shop on Melrose Avenue.

The BMX shop is called OnSomeShit.

When XXXTentacion shows up, he brings an entourage.

Including $ki Mask the Slump God, another Broward County rapper.

*

Talking about his criminal background, he makes four main points.

That he was arrested in his early youth for possession of a firearm, armed burglary, possession of OxyContin, grand theft, and resisting arrest without violence.

That he went to jail for a year.

That while in jail, he met $ki Mask.

That while in jail, he beat the shit out of a homosexual cellmate.

The final story is grotesque, involving XXXTentacion bashing in the kid's head and XXXTentacion taking the kid's blood and smearing it on his own face like warpaint.

The word faggot is employed with great frequency.

After the *No Jumper* interview, whenever a Righteous White writes about XXXTentacion, they will always include his year in jail, $ki Mask, and XXXTentacion's beating of a gay kid.

The homophobic beating signals itself to the Righteous: at long last, another Black dude who has disqualified himself from The Cause.

He's the latest and greatest find in that perpetual quest.

An African-American who can be criticized without anyone calling you racist.

The new O.J. Simpson.

And because Righteous Whites are nothing if not lazy, no one ever bothered to do any independent research.

No one verified a word that he said.

And it wasn't hard.

His Twitter had been there from the beginning, offering a definitive version of what happened.

And if you shell out $24, the Florida Department of Law Enforcement will sell you the barebones of his juvie record.

I paid that money.

And I don't even have a job!

*

As far as I can tell, very little of what he says on *No Jumper* is true.

And this is unusual.

Like I said in the previous chapter: everything about his use of social media, at least until the arrests of 2016 AD, makes it clear that this is a person of unusual honesty.

He's that dude.

The one who won't shut up.

The one who relates everything in laborious detail.

The best joke in Chris Rock's *Top 5* goes like this: "Richard Pryor is like the most honest human being ever… Even Jesus didn't tell his followers everything."

I can suggest another candidate.

*

The timeline is as follows.

He's arrested on 14 April 2013 AD.

He's picked up on charges of carrying a concealed firearm, possession of burglary weapons with intent to use, and armed burglary.

Of the other charges he mentions on *No Jumper*, I can find no evidence in this arrest.

*

He gets twenty-one days in juvenile detention.

On 5 May 2013 AD, he's released.

For two days.

On 7 May 2013 AD, he is sentenced to a year in bootcamp and is immediately shipped to its facility.

It is there that he meets $ki Mask the Slump God.

*

$ki Mask's real name is Stokeley Goulbourne.

He too is from Broward County.

They share a room.

XXXTentacion calls it a cell.

They start talking about how to get out of their shitty lives.

The timing is auspicious.

On 29 March 2013 AD, only a few weeks before his arrest, Jahseh Onfroy is tweeting at Chief Keef: "@ChiefKeef I got something i want you to listen to"

At the time, Chief Keef is the Internet rapper du jour.

*

This tweet is the first public indication, anywhere, that Jahseh Onfroy is interested in music.

Or making it.

And then he goes inside.

And meets $ki Mask the God.

With whom he will spend the next four years forming hip-hop collectives, making music, and performing.

*

XXXTentacion reemerges on 11 June 2013 AD.

He's got a two week furlough.

Following this reemergence, his third tweet is to $ki Mask.

It says: "@Hurt_God ugly mofo."

On 15 June 2013 AD, he tweets out a link to a snippet of a song.

It's the first time that Jahseh Onfroy has made his music available to the world.

On 16 June 2013 AD, he tweets again at $ki Mask: "@Hurt_God ya aunty eat ass, ayee you wanna slide to the studio"

On 18 June 2013 AD, he tweets a link at $ki Mask.

He links a song that he's just uploaded on SoundCloud.

It's called "News/Flock."

*

SoundCloud is a platform that has been around since 2008 AD.

People make music, or sounds, and upload their creative output.

Other people can listen to this creative output.

Like most things funded by Silicon Valley venture capitalists, SoundCloud has never turned a profit.

*

At roughly the same time that XXXTentacion gets on SoundCloud, a handful of other weirdo rappers are also uploading their music to the platform.

This later becomes useful as it suggests something that is catnip to journalists.

The impression of a trend.

Despite having almost nothing in common, other than being on SoundCloud, which technically could describe about twelve thousand people, this select group will be known as SoundCloud Rappers.

On 26 June 2013 AD, XXXTentacion goes back to bootcamp.

On 10 August 2013 AD, he returns home.

He's been kicked out.

And these two and a half months—three months and a week, if you count his twenty-one days predisposition—is the entirety of time that he does in anything like a correctional facility as a juvenile offender.

If you want to understand how bad the journalism about XXXTentacion has been, this is the place to think about it.

If you're a juvenile offender in Florida, and you aren't tried as an adult, it's impossible to go to prison for a year.

Juvenile prisons don't exist in Florida.

There are secure detention centers, which serve as pre-trial holding centers, and there are outsourced residential facilities, some of which are secure.

But there is no prison.

By 1 June 2013 AD, $ki Mask was back on Twitter.

Out of pokey.

Given the lack of tweets on $ki Mask's Twitter between November 2012 AD and June 2013 AD, it seems a safe inference that he was resident at the bootcamp long before XXXTentacion arrived.

Their time together overlapped by roughly a month.

•

This is the dark magic of the arts.

Everything is timing.

And everything is feeling.

And you have no control over when they two will meet.

•

There's no record of the homophobic beating.

It doesn't mean that it didn't happen.

Everything I know about Florida juvenile detention comes from the *Miami Herald*'s 2017 AD series of investigative reports about the conditions into which the state thrusts its youthful offenders.

Considering the overwhelming concern that America expresses for its poor and dispossessed, it may surprise you to learn that these conditions are barbaric and inhuman.

The title of the series was "Fight Club."

On 13 January 2014 AD, he tweets: "@nasty_doee did a month in the jail, than did 6 months in a boot camp, but i got kicked out so im just chillig now"

On 23 February 2014 AD, he tweets: "lol i served 7 months for robbing your house and fucking your bitch"

These are the only instances amongst his 27,000 tweets, prior to the 2016 AD arrests, where I can find a lie.

There are shadings of the truth, there are rhetorical exaggerations.

But actual lies?

Almost none.

So when he does lie, it's remarkable.

And telling.

Because he only lies about one thing: thug life.

When he's a lonely teenager and he has no fans.

When no one is watching.

An adolescent boy who wants to be perceived as hard on social media.

*

And it's completely unnecessary.

XXXTentacion was incredibly violent.

There's a million videos on the Internet of him beating the shit out of people.

*

Two types fight different than everyone else.

People who've done martial training and people who had awful childhoods.

You can spot the latter in an instant.

They're the ones who get into a schoolyard scrap and end up sticking a pen in someone's eye.

They go from 0 to 60 in less than a second.

They don't stop.

The violence is a familiar moment when the world can be reduced and be made sane.

XXXTentacion was one of these people.

He had pathological violence.

And he knew it.

*

9 May 2015 AD: "I don't want anyone to look at me like some ignorant violent ass nigga cause im not."

19 May 2015 AD: "I realized I have to force myself to be humane, less violent, to speak more, to love."

28 July 2015 AD: "I hate how violent I am, it scares me."

*

But given the fact that a smashed in head necessitates medical attention, and given the fact that I can find no mention of the incident anywhere in his tweets, and given the fact that the injuries as stated by XXXTentacion would have generated the sort of incident report on which the *Miami Herald* based "Fight Club," and given the fact that after he became famous no one claimed to be his victim in an era when the combination of victimhood and fame is the most alluring of poisons, and given that the story emerged during an interview where XXXTentacion flat out lies, I find it improbable that it occurred how he related it.

If it occurred at all.

*

And yet.

$ki Mask sat beside XXXTentacion during the *No Jumper* interview, and he seems to know what his friend is talking about.

But he also pretends that XXXTentacion spent a year in jail.

CHAPTER 4

Ò TU ÉTAIS UN VAMPIRE, ET BÉBÈ MOI JE MARCHE MORT

Imagine your drunk ass cousin.

At a wedding.

She's singing "I Will Always Love You."

Even if by some miracle she hits all the notes, she'll never sound like Whitney Houston.

*

Melody is the series of notes that carries a song through.

It's essentially the top of the song, the tune that you hum.

Harmony is the sound of all the different instruments together.

Rhythm is the beat and the way that the beat manifests itself across a piece of music.

It's the groove.

Lyrics are lyrics.

*

Timbre, roughly speaking, is everything in music that doesn't fall into the above four categories.

Timbre is what made Whitney Houston sound like Whitney Houston.

Timbre is what made Whitney Houston an international star.

And timbre is why your cousin only sings at weddings.

*

Rap is almost entirely rhythm and timbre.

Which means it's based in individual performance.

The idea of an individual performance of music having its own intrinsic reproducible value—as opposed to its merit being the underlying composition—is new enough that prior to the Copyright Act of 1972 AD, you couldn't copyright a recording of a musical performance with the United States Government.

The scored music underlying the performance?

Yes, you could copyright the composition.

But the individual performance?

No.

You could protect it through a patchwork of state law.

But not with Big Daddy.

*

And the idea of a copyrightable composition was defined, primarily, by melody and lyrics.

If through a miracle of time and space, XXXTentacion had recorded "Look At Me!" in 1971 AD, the lyrics would've been the only thing copyrightable with the United States Government.

Not the performance.

Not the backing melody, which is sampled from "Changes" by Mala.

Not the rhythm.

Not the distortion.

Not the beat.

It's a song with no topline and no harmony.

I don't understand arcane law enough to say whether or not lyrics unaccompanied by a top-line melody could have been copyrighted at as musical composition.

They might have had to be copyrighted as a poem.

LOOK AT ME!

FUCK ON ME!

© 1971 Jahseh Onfroy.

*

By the way, this is a perfect example of what people mean when they talk about systemic racism.

*

This isn't just an XXXTentacion thing.

This is hip-hop.

There from the beginning.

Spoken rhymes over break beats on turn tables.

*

"Revenge" is an XXXTentacion song that resembles what the people who write copyright laws think of as a song.

There's a melody, there's harmony, there's sung lyrics, something like verses and a chorus, and not too much of an emphasis on groove.

The music and vocals are jaunty, playing against the lyrics in which the song's protagonist wonders whether or not he should act out revenge against an ex-lover by putting both her and himself in a set of pre-dug graves.

On 18 January 2016 AD, XXXTentacion tweets: "If you actually thoroughly listen to my music, you'll realize im not a rapper."

"Revenge" is the proof of this statement.

This song is as far from rap as you can get.

*

In almost the exact opposite direction is "schizophrenia."

It has no chorus, no harmony, barely a melody, and a bizarre three-part structure.

It begins with XXXTentacion whispering about voices being heard in the head, segues into a guitar-driven middle with XXXTentacion doing lead vocals like someone in a Manchester post-punk band of the early 1980s AD, and then crashes into XXXTentacion screaming "Don't give up!" about twenty times.

*

Many of his early SoundCloud songs are three minutes or longer.

As he went on, the songs got shorter and shorter.

"schizophrenia" was released a few months before that bullet hit his neck.

It's one minute and twenty seconds long.

It's the perfect length.

Long enough to assault you, but too short to ever leave the listener with the sense that they can catch the song.

There's never enough to grasp.

You're left wanting more.

And like "Revenge," it's as far as you can get from rap.

*

"Find Me (Intro)" is the first track off *Members Only, Vol. 3.*

Members Only, Vol. 3 was the third, and sole commercial, release of the eponymous Broward County hip-hop collective founded by XXXTentacion.

The rest of the album is a showcase for the wild flows and production skills of the collective, with an emphasis on noise, gross-out humor and distortion.

"Find Me (Intro)" is the strangest possible introduction to the rest of the material.

It sounds like it'd be more at home on *17.*

17 was XXXTentacion's first commercially released studio album.

In an interview with XXL, XXXTentacion described *17* as belonging to the Internet-invented genre of alternative R&B.

*

Like all contemporary musical subgenres invented by the Internet, alternative R&B doesn't make a lot of sense when trying to find a connective link amongst the artists to whom it's applied.

It's little more than the vague suggestion that people are using new techniques to make songs that don't sound like bad cover versions of shit people recorded twenty years ago.

*

When XXXTentacion does his alternative R&B, his voice is beautiful in the same way that Bob Dylan's voice is beautiful.

This beauty is the underlying basis of all American musical greatness.

The beauty that self-styled connoisseurs of beauty cannot hear.

It's an old hillbilly down in a holler with a banjo.

It's the broken note on a side street.

It's your cousin singing Whitney Houston.

*

XXXTentacion sounds like a wounded animal that stays down.

He sounds like the saddest person in the world.

He sounds like someone who overdosed on The Weeknd's mixtapes and chased them with a dose of pure sorrow.

*

It's one of Those Voices.

There's probably twenty in the history of American recorded music.

Johnny Cash, Ol' Dirty Bastard, Etta James, Leadbelly.

The ones that cut through the technology.

That just are.

Aching with timbre.

*

The album art of *Vol. 3* quotes from a 31 January 2017 AD article posted on hotnewhiphop.com.

The article was called "Everything You Need to Know about XXXTENTACION."

It's a great example of the condensed biographical nonsense that passes for music writing.

Vaguely right but totally wrong.

The rough rare meat of your life goes into a machine and comes out as flavorless pink sludge.

The quote on *Vol. 3* goes like this:

> According to his own description, X was living the life of a "young savage" – correctional houses, grandma's house, robbing houses. He built up

> a formidable rap sheet: armed robbery, armed burglary, possession of a firearm, resisting arrest, three charges of grand theft, oxycodone possession. Cops found hollow-tipped bullets in his gun. He spent a year in jail. There he met Ski Mask the Slump God, a talented rapper with whom he quickly formed a close bond. Upon their release they teamed up with Wifisfuneral and Craig Xen to form the rap crew known as Members Only.

Speaking of Bob Dylan.

Whenever he'd play a gig in the 2000s AD, his stage manager would introduce the show by reading from an article that someone'd written for the *Buffalo News*.

This is what his manager would read:

> Ladies and gentlemen please welcome the poet laureate of rock 'n' roll. The voice of the promise of the 60's counterculture. The guy who forced folk into bed with rock. Who donned makeup in the 70's and disappeared into a haze of substance abuse. Who emerged to find Jesus. Who was written off as a has-been by the end of the 80's, and who suddenly shifted gears releasing some of the strongest music of his career beginning in the late 90's. Ladies and gentlemen—Columbia recording artist Bob Dylan!

Everything you need to know about Bob Dylan.

Nothing ever changes.

*

"UP LIKE AN INSOMNIAC" is a freestyle that ended up on *A Ghetto Christmas Carol*, an EP with a runtime of nine minutes and eight seconds.

There's no real melody, there's no harmony.

There's just a killer beat and with two verses and a one-line chorus repeated about fifty times: "BITCH, I AM UP."

The first verse is XXXTentacion moving though several different flows, delivered in cartoony voices.

But lots of people can rap in weird voices.

The second verse is where the unmistakable touch emerges.

Two different flows, each with their own delivery.

If you go to YouTube and watch people's reaction videos, it's the first flow that's the moment of shock.

Like a needle scratching off a record.

Because this is where XXXTentacion's screamo voice comes out about as hard and as effective as it was ever used.

It sounds like someone asked another Florida native, Glenn Benton, lead vocalist of seminal death metal band Deicide, to deliver a guest verse.

And, holy fuck, Glenn Benton is on point.

*

And this hints at an idea that I couldn't bother developing in this book, but wanted to get in anyway: the origins of death metal are Floridian.

Death, Deicide, Cannibal Corpse, Morbid Angel.

You can make a case that XXXTentacion's sonic unpleasantries, best encapsulated in that screamo voice, are the obvious inheritors of this geographic legacy.

*

The song proves something that isn't necessarily apparent when you first encounter XXXTentacion's music.

The guy could murder when he wanted.

*

The above four songs were chosen at random.

I'm suspicious of streaming audio quality, so I still fuck with .mp3 and .flac.

I dumped all my XXXTentacion into Winamp and decided to respond to the first four songs that came up.

*

In those four songs, selected at random by antiquated technology, you find XXXTentacion working across a wide range of genres, doing things that rappers have never done.

And there's never any doubt, not once, not in all the different voices and approaches, about who is performing.

He always sounds like himself.

*

Put this into perspective.

Until the day that human life ends, David Bowie will receive handjobs from the White commentariat regarding the glorious decade that he spent shape-shifting from one album to the next while maintaining a grand cohesive artistic unity.

If you listen to *A Ghetto Christmas Carol*, you'll find XXXTentacion doing the same thing.

Across five songs.

On the same album.

In nine minutes.

And eight seconds.

*

People used to think that rock n' roll was a revolutionary music.

No joke.

The reoccurring motif of four-to-five proletariat idiots with guitars and wah-wah pedals was conceived as a vanguard of a forthcoming social change.

This is why Jean-Luc Godard, then in high Maoist mode, spent 1968 AD shooting films with The Jefferson Airplane and The Rolling Stones.

The funniest artifact of this mentality is an advertisement that CBS/Columbia Records ran in the late 1960s AD:

The person who started this delusion, accidentally, was Bob Dylan.

Who was also on Columbia Records.

It wasn't his fault.

He just wanted to make some music.

But there was something about his lyrics and the two years that he spent positioning himself as part of a presumed Radical Left.

Everyone ended up convinced of the inherent revolutionary potential within rock.

And that his songs meant something, man.

You can see this in the sheer number of books written about the guy.

They tally in the hundreds, if not the thousands.

With the exception of two books by Greil Marcus, they're all fucking terrible.

•

From the earliest, people make arguments for the significance of the lyrics and their meaning, and write very little about the fact that these words were delivered in the context of music.

Without any disrespect to Dylan, who is the great American genius of the Twentieth Century AD, what he managed to do not was not write anthemic songs of protest and existential ballads of life in the United States, but find the appropriate sound to deliver those lyrics.

The lyrics are the least important thing with Dylan.

It's all phraseology, it's all timbre.

He could have been singing anything.

•

After Taylor Swift released her album *1989*, Ryan Adams released a song-by-song cover album.

It's also called *1989*.

It includes "Welcome to New York," which was the second single from Swift's *1989*.

Adams's version of "Welcome to New York" sounds like crap Bruce Springsteen.

After Ryan Adams did his *1989*, Father John Misty covered Ryan Adams's version of "Welcome to New York."

Misty did it in the style of the early Velvet Underground.

And unlike Ryan Adams's crap Bruce Springsteen, Misty's Velvet Underground sounds pitch perfect.

He nails that VU sound.

The sound transforms "Welcome to New York."

It leaves behind Taylor Swift's vacuous celebration of Russian oligarchs getting a little tipsy, and maybe doing a bump of coke in the Momofuku bathroom.

And it becomes the old New York.

The titular line, the welcoming to the city, sounds like Quentin Crisp asking you to cop dope down on Avenue A & 3rd.

*

Like everyone in popular music, the Velvet Underground were defined by timbre.

By ambiance.

That's the trick.

All you have to do is find the sound.

*

XXXTentacion understood, consciously or not, that if hip-hop as a culture is different than the genre of rap, and if that culture emerged from a musical style determined entirely by timbre and performance, then if you came from hip-hop you could do anything and still be hip-hop.

And he also realized that rap is the culmination of a certain tendency in American popular music.

The interchangeable folk idiom there from the beginning and reemerging up after recording technology murdered Tin Pan Alley.

It had always been about the sound.

Timbre is the most important thing.

It's the only thing.

*

And the key description in the above section is "popular music."

*

Garage bands were the SoundCloud trap of their era.

The cheapest place you could go when you wanted to become famous and express yourself even if you didn't, necessarily, have any talent.

An entire generation of people wanted to be Mick Jagger.

And almost none of them ever made it.

Finding a sound is even harder than reducing yourself into a reproducible icon of mass culture.

Some people are born with it.

Some people develop it.

Most people who have it will eventually lose it.

After 1972 AD, not even Mick Jagger was Mick Jagger.

*

The radicality of rap has always freaked people out.

From the beginning.

You can see this in the academic quest to find its antecedents.

The griot, pimp toasts, cultural memory.

The underlying idea being: if we can explain this new thing through the application of history, then we don't have to worry about its legitimacy.

I suspect that this discomfort emerges from a truly radical idea emerging amongst the poorest people in America and being dependent upon their vernacular.

*

The disquietude has fueled its own paradox.

No genre of American music has been given greatest emphasis on lyricism, and lyrical constraints and finesse, than rap.

But the amount of people who actually give a fuck about lyricism is small and ever diminishing.

Remember The KLF's *Manual.*

If you want to have a hit song, make sure that the chorus expresses one universal sentiment, hammer it over and over again, and don't worry about the verses having any meaning.

Verse, chorus, verse, chorus, bridge, chorus, chorus, chorus.

That's how you get the plague of Macklemore.

*

And that's the genius of XXXTentacion.

And make no mistake.

He was a genius.

Fuck a chorus.

Fuck a verse.

Fuck every known song structure.

Fuck every received idea about music.

While remaining popular.

While remaining danceable.

Because otherwise it's just Norwegian Black Metal.

*

The fundamental argument of rap, that culminating tendency in American music, taken to its furthest known extension.

All the way back to Harlem World.

To Sedgwick Avenue.

And sounding nothing like it.

Delivered in that voice.

The wounded radical.

CHAPTER 5

PROBATION

The remainder of 2013 AD is preparation for the life that's going to hit him in two years.

Despite getting kicked out of bootcamp, he's allowed to continue with his probation.

And then summer's over.

And school starts.

·

Two of his saddest tweets are from this moment.

They're both on the same day.

30 August 2013 AD.

The first goes: "anyone know any alternative high schools besides whiddon and dave thomas ?"

The second goes: "anyone know any alternative schools"

*

It's idiotic to engage in counterhistorical speculation.

But.

If the Jahseh Onfroy of 2013 AD was anything, then he was the perfect candidate for an alternative education.

Fucked up, artistically oriented, desperate for the meaningful connections that a normal classroom makes impossible, and someone chronically incapable of functioning in anything like a systematized education environment.

The poster boy.

And the world has failed him so badly that he's asking for help from stoned teenagers on Twitter.

*

He doesn't end up in alternative education.

He attends Piper High School, in Sunrise, which has almost three thousand students.

*

Perhaps not unrelated: this period involves him taking a startling amount of drugs.

And this is a generational thing, too.

For decades, drug use had balanced between people having genuine fun and the pathetic blotting out of the self.

Somewhere in the late '90s, the balance shifted toward the latter.

In a way, this was another governmental conspiracy.

Because someone had to approve the voracious lust of Big Pharma.

And someone had to say yes to the idea of an entire population enslaved by medication.

And so one of the better ideas from the Twentieth Century AD was poisoned.

The pathetic blotting out of the self became the de facto approach.

*

Jahseh Onfroy's emerged from the corrections system and all he's doing is getting fucked the fuck up.

A different kind of poster boy.

In the months that follow bootcamp, he's eating, smoking or snorting the following: cocaine, morphine, unnamed pills, weed, molly, LSD, Xanax, alcohol, Oxycontin, opium, bath salts, Adderall.

He's fifteen and sixteen years old.

Party on.

*

Somewhere between 25 September 2013 AD and 28 September 2013 AD, he changes his Twitter account.

@fuckjahseh dies.

And @xxxtentacion is born.

*

It's got that thing required by every mass market product.

It has that *what the fuck* factor.

The first time you encounter it, it's inscrutable and confusing.

By the fifth time, it's natural.

By the tenth, it's always been there.

On 9 October 2013 AD he tweets: "no one understand my twitter name, it means 'sexual' or 'pornographic' temptation."

And much later, on May 5, 2015 AD: "the name 'xxxtentacion' is completely original, it's about my habit or 'temptations' to do crazy or erotic things, Triple X , Temptation."

*

He releases more music on SoundCloud.

*

December of 2013 AD is bad.

On 9 December, get gets kicked out his house.

And he gets suspended from Piper.

Two days later, he's arrested for possession of a controlled substance without a prescription.

He's put on house arrest.

Four days on an ankle monitor.

*

2014 AD begins.

There's a tension: is Jahseh Onfroy, a person suffering every serious systemic disadvantage, going to follow the script of his life?

Or can this rap shit actually do something?

*

In January, prosecutors drop the concealed weapon charge from his original 2013 AD arrest.

Then there's more drugs, more fighting with his family, more getting kicked out and let back in.

*

On 19 February 2014 AD, he's expelled from Piper.

Thus ends his formal education.

*

Now he has what every artist needs.

He has time.

For all the normal teenage shit: drugs, fucking, violence.

But also for music.

On the first day of March, he buys a microphone.

By the 5th, he's released his first mixtape.

On SoundCloud.

It's called *XXX*.

He's so unknown that no one saves a copy.

And because he has the habit of deleting his music—usually from total dissatisfaction with its quality—all of the songs on *XXX* are lost.

*

On 17 May 2014 AD, he's arrested under FS 856.021.

Loitering or Prowling.

No way to tell which.

He's carrying some weed, which gets him a possession charge.

Just like his father.

He spends three nights in jail and then is released on house arrest.

The charges eventually come to nothing.

*

House arrest lasts into June.

Around this time, he really starts fucking with Nirvana.

He tweets a few times about Kurt Cobain.

Pop music's most beautiful suicide, complete in every detail.

It's the beginning of an obsession.

Later, when people have started paying attention, XXXTentacion will talk about Kurt Cobain being his major influence.

*

And then something very strange happens.

*

Between 16 July 2014 AD and 31 December 2014 AD, there are no available tweets.

This is the only mystery of his account, the only unexplained absence.

Every other gap is explicable.

*

If you search for people tweeting at him during this period, it's clear that he was still active on the platform.

People are responding to his tweets.

We have to assume that deleting these tweets was a deliberate act.

It's unclear why.

It is more than possible that something very terrible happened during this time.

*

In the middle of this mystery, we arrive at what will haunt XXXTentacion for the last two years of his life.

His relationship with the young woman calling herself Geneva Sativa.

*

In October 2016 AD, XXXTentacion is arrested for allegedly beating and kidnapping her.

This arrest will poison his name in every possible way.

If the *No Jumper* podcast is kindling, then this arrest is the match.

But we'll get to that later.

*

Just before the bullet hit his neck, the *Miami New Times* ran an article written by an editorial intern under the headline "The Real Story of South Florida Rapper XXXTentacion."

It is poorly researched.

But it's valuable because it's the only place where you can find Geneva being interviewed and talking about her relationship with XXXTentacion.

Geneva pinpoints the exact day that she met XXXTentacion.

25 November 2014 AD.

Right in the middle of the inexplicable break on his Twitter.

They hung out together for about half a week.

And then they didn't see each other for almost two years.

*

Also during the blank period, he gets arrested.

He's picked up on charges of giving law enforcement a false name.

This is on 30 September 2014 AD.

The charges get dropped on 14 October 2014 AD.

*

And then, on December 30th, his tweets are back.

Just in time for 2015 AD.

He mentions an upcoming show on the 21st of March.

*

January is one of those months.

On the 6th, he tweets that he's going to be arrested soon.

On the 9th, he's arrested.

The charges are possession of burglary tools with intent to use, resisting arrest without violence, and loitering and prowling.

Here's something that we must consider: it's possible that throughout this whole time, as he's transforming himself into a pop sensation, he's also robbing houses.

The charges are all dropped by March.

*

He's on house arrest from the 12th of January until the 31st.

A few new themes arrive on his Twitter.

He's got a new girlfriend.

She'll be around for a while.

She seems like his first real love other than maybe a girl he was fucking when he first opened his Twitter account.

And his taste in music is expanding.

Here's what he's listening to: Teen Suicide, Patti Smith, Ariel Pink, Lorde, Bon Iver, Movado, Suicide Doros, Amy Winehouse, Hozier, Teddy Blow.

If a White boy were listening to this list, no one would blink.

But whenever a Black person stumbles upon the anthems of the ruling class, which is to say punk and indie rock, there's a music journalist waiting to say that the person's influences are wide-ranging and eclectic.

•

On 21 March 2015 AD, he plays his first real show.

It's called #RedWallMarch21st and it's hosted by White Wall FL.

Here's the event description:

> **WWFLA PRESENTS: #REDWALLMARCH21ST.**
>
> **#RedWallMarch21st** - The event will take place March 21. Come out, enjoy music, drinks, WAVY gear from hot local brands and a personal/group photo on the Red-Wall by the best photographers in South Florida!
>
> **Adding Kodak camera's to the event! Take pictures of the day you had. When the event ends , Drop off the Kodak in an envelope with your email address and we'll get the pictures sent to you!**

Shot by: @Daykuul @Mr.TopNotch, @Brandon Dali & Our Guests.

Performances by: Xali, Shark Anthony, Zaymatic, WifisFuneral, Emily Cleary, Chief Oyabun, Nobodies, ATG103, Whxte Mike, Rapper Rich, Mike Merrill, Casey Jones, The Cool Era.

DOONEY MONTANA - Smart Stunnas (PERFORMANCE DEBUT)

RANSOOO ROCKCHILD- Art Klub

TREY XAVIER - ShakeDown

WIFISFUNERAL - West Palm Beach

AVIANT REDZ - Broward County

DREW SKI, Rshad Joh, Ya$, SP, Nick Owens, DXDDYMXCK , DelmarJFK, King kev, Jiggy Mane The Plug, Noex, Norah Johnson, xxxTentation & more.

*

From his tweets, I get the sense that his set went well.

*

Here wee should pause and think about the distinction between Jahseh Onfroy and XXXTentacion.

It's like two living beings in one body.

XXXTentacion is transcendent, radiant.

He's the inner core.

He can't be stopped.

In less than two years, he'll be on the *Billboard* charts with a song that was uploaded to SoundCloud.

And then there's Jahseh Onfroy.

Jahseh Onfroy's life was marked by the blunt reality that he had terrible luck.

Whenever anything could go wrong, it did.

It's a defining aspect of his existence.

And like anyone with bad luck, a great deal of it was self-inflicted.

•

The inner radiant core is unstoppable.

But it's housed in a born loser.

And he's getting very, very close to being famous.

A person with awful luck is about to be pulled into unfathomable success.

Someone to whom nothing good ever happens is on the verge of having all his dreams come true.

•

But that's a few months away.

Right now, XXXTentacion has finished playing his first real show.

He seems happy.

And then Jahseh Onfroy takes the wheel.

Almost immediately after his performance, he gets jumped by another rapper and that rapper's crew.

This is a beating that he didn't see coming.

Only a few hours earlier, he had a warm encounter with the other rapper.

They fuck him up.

They fuck up his girl and hurt her eye.

*

The rest of the spring and summer are the same as the last few months.

The music is getting better.

He's getting well known.

He's getting recognized when he goes outside.

He's playing more shows.

*

In that *Miami New Times* article, Geneva says that after those few days of intense contact, she and XXXTentacion didn't see each other again until 2016 AD.

But there's a tweet from 19 May 2015 AD.

It says one word.

"Geneva"

Who knows?

*

On 25 November 2015 AD, he gets off probation.

Earlier, he tweets: "I finish my probation in two weeks, I've been on probation for three years, I'm proud of myself!"

And: "went from robbing niggas houses, check scams , snatching chains and pawning shit to making money off saying a few words with meaning."

*

The insane thing is that on 16 November 2015 AD, he goes out and robs a dude.

For this particular crime, he won't be arrested until nearly a year later.

*

It goes down like this.

He and three other individuals go into someone's house.

XXXTentacion hits the dude in the head with a pistol.

They steal an iPad, an iPhone, a Sony PSP, and $20.

*

He's really close to being free of the criminal justice system.

He's tweeting about how happy he is to be away from its contretemps and how he's proud of getting through the program.

And he's going out and pulling some small time shit.

*

And here's that Jahseh Onfroy luck again: when he's charged with this crime, it turns out that his victim identified him from a photo of XXXTentacion on Twitter.

*

On 30 December 2015 AD, a new song is uploaded to SoundCloud.

It's called "Look At Me!"

It's a fucking monster.

It will do that thing which every artist hopes every new release will do.

But which never happens.

It will change his life.

In slightly over a year, "Look At Me!" will bubble up onto the *Billboard* charts.

When it happens, he'll be in jail.

CHAPTER 6

#UNEXPECETD CONSEQUENCZ!

By the time of the .mp3's blossoming, the recording industry was like all American culture production.

It had consolidated into a handful of companies under the iron fist of the same people who own everything.

These companies were called The Big Six.

Every major recording artist in America worked for these companies.

In the twenty years since the dawn of the .mp3, The Big Six have become The Big Three.

Warner Music Group, which is owned by a Russian oligarch.

Sony Music Entertainment, which is owned by
Sony Corporation of America, which is owned by
Sony Corporation, a Tokyo-based Japanese conglomerate.

Universal Music Group, which is owned by Vivendi, a French media conglomerate.

•

When the .mp3 hit, Sony was in a strange position.

It manufactured music.

But it also manufactured electronics.

This introduced an incoherence into their response to new technology.

On one hand, the music division did not want its media pirated.

On the other hand, the electronics division could make a ton of money if it sold devices that were .mp3 enabled.

Do you manufacture electronics at the expense of the golden goose?

The answer didn't matter.

The psychopath Steve Jobs came in and sat on everyone.

Apple made iPods.

And then Apple made iTunes.

And then the recording industry was, for the first time in a very long time, riding in the backseat.

*

For decades, success in recorded music has been measured by the *Billboard* sales charts.

The two charts that mattered were the *Top 200 Albums* and the *Hot 100*.

The *Hot 100* measured the popularity of songs.

The *Top 200* measured the popularity of albums.

*

The *Billboard* charts are like the Oscars: a meaningless American institution that shapes our shared social reality.

They're how your masters keep you in control.

Pretend like it fucking matters.

*

But a tool only works as well as its design.

In 1991 AD, *Billboard* switched over to SoundScan.

SoundScan was point-of-sale measurement.

Prior to its advent, music sales numbers were imaginary, made up by dishonest distributors and bribed retailers.

After SoundScan, a stunning reality emerged.

People really liked to fuck with recordings made by Black people.

It's possible that the known history of sales up until 1991 AD was a web of lies designed to hide the financial and cultural impact of Black people.

The Funky Tramp, a comedy album by Jimmy Lynch, sold over a million copies.

It never showed up on any *Billboard* chart.

In 2005 AD, *Billboard* incorporated digital downloads into its methodology of tallying popularity.

By this time, the *Hot 100* was everything.

iTunes and piracy had murdered albums.

Singles were back.

Two years later, in 2007 AD, *Billboard* changed its chart methodology to incorporate online streaming music.

This meant almost nothing.

There were no services that anyone used.

Billboard only tracked music streamed by AOL and Yahoo!

For the record: these companies no longer exist.

Having been burned by piracy and iTunes, The Big Three muscled in on streaming.

They negotiated deals with the major services.

Providers like Pandora and Spotify were allowed to stream music from Sony and Warners and Universal.

The providers would pay royalties on these streams.

The royalties were structured in a particularly cruel way.

They were almost nothing.

Fractional cents per stream.

If you were an individual artist, you'd have to generate an enormous amount of streams to make any money.

But The Big Three would get a cut of each stream.

And, in the aggregate, reap huge rewards.

*

As part of the negotiations, the Big Three were given minority ownership stakes in the streaming companies with which they negotiated paltry royalties.

They bought equity in potential future payouts by accepting smaller royalties for the artists who made the music.

*

After The Big Three took ownership stakes in streaming services, these services began to be included in *Billboard* charts.

This was both a business arrangement designed to increase the value of those ownership stakes and a necessary response to the imaginarium of the Internet.

The digital world had wreaked more havoc.

People had stopped paying for individual downloads.

*

The revised methodology for the *Top 200 Albums* chart worked like this: ten streams were considered the equivalent of a single song sale, and fifteen hundred streams were considered the equivalent of an album sale.

For the *Hot 100*, the methodology was less exact: sales accounted for 35-45% of a song's performance, radio airplay for 30-40%, and streaming for 20-30%.

*

None of the streaming services turned a profit.

Their earned revenues evaporated into royalties, cost of operations, and ad-sharing payments.

*

If your customer base is unwilling to pay for your product, and the people who rule the world have disincentivized your customers from ever giving you money again, then it's time to figure out a new way of doing business.

New releases were reoriented around streaming.

Think about Drake's 2016 AD album *Views*.

That motherfucking thing has twenty tracks!

When seventy-five people stream that album in its entirety, it counts as an album equivalent sale.

If enough of these streams happen, it'll get the album on the *Billboard* charts.

Which will generate endless press coverage.

Which will keep the release on the *Billboard* charts.

Which will generate more press coverage.

Which will increase streams.

And each time one of those twenty tracks is streamed, it pays a royalty, and the user growth of the streaming service will increase the perceived value a minority ownership stake in the service on which the track is streamed.

And if the last ten years have proved anything, there's millions of people who'll waste their lives streaming Drake.

*

In November 2014 AD, Warner did an equity and licensing deal with SoundCloud.

In January 2016 AD, Universal did an equity and licensing deal with SoundCloud.

In March 2016 AD, Sony did an equity and licensing deal with SoundCloud.

*

In October 2016 AD, *Billboard* began including streams from SoundCloud in its methodology.

It wasn't every song on the service.

Only songs that had been monetized.

*

According to a tweet, 23 April 2016 AD was the day when SoundCloud began monetizing XXXTentacion's music.

*

After the inclusion of streaming, the *Hot 100* became about the bargain between the American public, the investor/entrepreneurial classes, and the music industry.

We will throw money at artists and record labels, said the investor/entrepreneurial class, i*n the form of royalties in the hopes that one day these investments will pay off through the perceived value of user growth.*

We will give you user growth, said the American public, *as long as you don't ask us to pay money while we destroy our brains with the ghostwritten output of Drake.*

We have always been, we will always be, said the record labels. *We have the survivability of cockroaches. Free money sounds great. And fuck the artists.*

*

But messing around with complex systems always produces unexpected consequences.

And that's XXXTentacion.

An unexpected result of the bargain made between The Big Three, *Billboard*, and SoundCloud.

Sheer talent and a rabid fanbase could inflict "Look At Me!" onto the national consciousness.

Because that *Hot 100* chart is everything.

It determines reality.

And for a moment, the window was open.

*

When XXXTentacion broke onto the *Hot 100*, it was on the chart dated February 25, 2017 AD chart.

It was published on Valentine's Day 2017 AD.

More than a full calendar year after "Look At Me!" was first uploaded.

The chart was a compilation of streaming and digital downloads dated 3 February to 9 February, and radio plays dated 6 February to 12 February.

*

In terms of XXXTentacion, radio play doesn't really matter.

That shit wasn't being rocked on the radio.

In terms of digital downloads, kworb.net estimates that "Look At Me!" sold about 3,000 units, making it roughly the 200th best-selling track on iTunes.

Which leaves streaming.

For the week ending 10 February, which includes a full extra day, "Look At Me!" was streamed 1,779,340 times on Spotify.

There's no data on Apple Music or Amazon Music Unlimited.

Pandora wasn't yet included in tabulating the Hot 100.

Which leaves SoundCloud.

I can verify an actual number of SoundCloud streams for the week in question.

2,368,368.

This isn't all the plays.

It's the best I can do.

An unverifiable number, put together through guess work, is 2,736,993.

*

"Look At Me!" made its first appearance on the *Hot 100* at #95.

Without radio support, without a huge number of digital downloads, without (I suspect) a huge presence on Apple Music, and with streaming account for at most

30% of the tallying, XXXTentacion clawed his way onto the charts.

That's where those 2,736,993 streams matter.

When you're at the bottom, you're doing that marginal, fractional math.

*

Some people show up on the *Billboard Hot 100* and no one even notices.

But XXXTentacion'd been bubbling underground for months.

And the Billboard charts manufacture our shared reality, which means they're written about, and considered, as part of the great neoliberal consensus.

And, remember, for at least forty years, that consensus has been this: morality is indistinguishable from success.

*

By the time that XXXTentacion arrived, he'd done that *No Jumper* interview and he'd been arrested for allegedly beating Geneva Sativa.

Any appearance on the charts was going to create a serious disconnect between the illusion of the *Hot 100*'s meaning and an accidental manifestation of its actual function.

And that would generate coverage.

And that would generate commentary.

And that would generate further streams.

*

Those streams of "Look At Me!" were happening on platforms that were minority-owned by The Big Three, so in theory they were adding value to investments.

But the streams also represented something in direct opposition to The Big Three.

An unfiltered independent recording artist climbing into mainstream life.

Who had a very difficult and checkered history.

*

And if you wonder how his unexpected ascent was received, you need only think about one thing.

People like making money, but they hate being embarrassed.

We live in a world where the rich are kept in check by the threat of difficult questions at dinner parties.

*

In May 2017 AD, *Billboard* announced that it would yet again change the methodology of its charts:

> Beginning with the first week of Nielsen's third quarter of 2018... plays on paid subscription-based services (such as Apple Music and Amazon Music) or on the paid subscription tiers of hybrid paid/ad-supported platforms (such as Spotify and SoundCloud) will be given more weight in chart calculations than plays on ad-supported services (such as YouTube) or on the non-paid tiers of hybrid paid/ad-supported services.

> Billboard will have multiple weighted tiers of streaming plays for the Hot 100, which take into account paid subscription streams (representing a full point value per play), ad-supported streams (representing a 2/3-point value per play) and programmed streams (representing a 1/2-point value per play). Those values are then applied to the chart's formula alongside all-genre radio airplay and digital song sales data. Streaming remains the most dominant factor on the chart, followed by radio airplay and digital sales in descending order of significance.

In other words: they'll never make that mistake again.

CHAPTER 7

SEXXX WITH WITCH3S

2016 AD begins.

It's the first time in his life where he seems happy.

He's off probation.

Which means that he can leave the state of Florida.

*

It starts with a road trip.

XXXTentacion, $ki Mask and three other dudes in Members Only drive to a gig in Denver, Colorado.

Three days on the road.

Florida→Georgia→Tennessee→Missouri→Kansas→Colorado.

The gig happens on 9 January.

While they're traveling, they shoot footage.

It gets edited down and released on YouTube.

Everyone's on some Jack Kerouac shit.

Happy, goofy, out discovering America.

When they get to that rocky mountain high of Colorado, these Floridian youths do the only natural thing.

They play in the snow.

*

But life is never easy.

After the gig, XXXTentacion gets into a fight.

He kicks the shit out of some kid.

The video ends up online.

*

This is the period where he starts doing live online video.

It's a way of chatting with fans, of extending an immediacy.

He's also playing a lot of video games, and inviting his admirers to network with him on PlayStation Live.

*

Back in Florida, on 20 January, he gets into an altercation at Deerfield Beach.

9 JANUARY 2016 AD : DENVER

He stabs at least three people.

No one dies.

Without referring to the specifics of the event, he tweets about it: “bruh this shit real life, ya’ll niggas think this is a game, you try that tweaking shit ima stab the life out you.”

And: “how ya’ll 40 deep tryna jump me and don’t get shit done 😁, I aint take no L’s so far in 2016!”

·

In February, XXXTentacion decides to do an appearance tour of high school parking lots.

The proposed itinerary is Monarch, Coral Glades, and Deerfield.

On 22 February, at 2:25PM, he shows up at Monarch.

A few hours later, he tweets three times.

“I will not be able to attend your schools, apparently I have a warrant for my arrest, my apologies to everyone.”

“I searched the data base and nothing came up so I’m assuming the police are harassing me because of prior charges.”

“but if I am arrested at any point in time for a crime I did not commit, I did not kill myself”

Only on 3 March is it clear that there is no warrant.

·

He starts tweeting that Jahseh Onfroy is disappearing.

That Jahseh is being killed.

That soon there will only be X.

*

Meanwhile, "Look At Me!" is wracking up plays on SoundCloud.

By 7 March 2016 AD, it's over 500,000.

*

And then he's in Austin, Texas.

It's South by South West.

He performs with Joey Bada$$ and Denzel Curry at The House of Vans pop-up.

And, of course, he's got problems.

He tweets the following: "my first day out here I slapped someone, I really need to work on my temper."

*

In April, he spends a week in Los Angeles.

He gets paid $700 to appear in a porn video for a now-defunct website called *Groupie Lust*.

Groupie Lust's theme is this: pornstars hang around with barely known rappers.

Then the pornstars generally fuck someone other than the rapper.

XXXTentacion played it different than the other barely known rappers.

He fucked a woman on camera for eventual Internet distribution.

Which isn't that different from the content on his SnapChat or his Twitter dick picks.

In any case, his *Groupie Lust* video is never released.

Lost treasure rarity!

*

Watching videos from *Groupie Lust* is the second worst research conducted for this book.

There are many things I need in my life.

Here is something that I do not: watching $ki Mask the Slump God spit bars next to a couch where a girl's going reverse cowgirl.

*

Also while he's in Los Angeles: XXXTentacion does the *No Jumper* appearance, which isn't released until he's out of town.

Also while he's in Los Angeles: "Look At Me!" hits a million plays.

Also while he's in Los Angeles: SoundCloud starts paying him for his music.

Then he goes to Portland, Oregon.

He's there for about a week.

He gets fucked by a witch, arguably the only reason to ever go to Oregon.

He plays a show at an indoor skatepark in the suburb of Clackamas.

The flyer looks like this:

*

It's worth thinking about these experiences.

Until now, he's been trapped in Florida.

First by extreme youth, second by the criminal justice system.

And now he can leave.

And he's touring.

Until you've done it, you can't understand touring.

Not even that awful Bob Seger song can convey the strangeness.

You're sleeping in unfamiliar places, you're meeting business contacts without whom you'll be lost in unknown places, and the fans are all very nice but intrusive and have thought about you more than you could ever possibly think about them, and everybody wants something, and many of the people you meet will you give almost anything to get that something.

It's down the rabbit hole.

It's another reality.

Free drugs.

Sex with witches.

Life is nothing but a dream.

You can't remember your old existence.

Goodbye the banal experiences of your day-to-day.

Everything seems thin, like the border between reality and fantasy is a wet piece of paper that you can poke your finger through.

And then you have to go home.

And nothing has changed.

All the same problems are still there.

All the same faces.

And then, after an arbitrary period of time, you have to go out and repeat the experience.

*

For even the most stable of individuals, this is unmooring.

And it was happening to Jahseh Onfroy.

Who was nuts.

*

When he heads back to Florida, it's a countdown to the end.

The first thing he does is play the CitrusRap Stage at Rolling Loud.

*

He runs a contest on Twitter to see who can play his music the loudest in a classroom.

7 MAY 2016 AD: MIAMI

It's Part Two of that aborted parking lot tour.

Many fans respond with videos of "Look at Me!" being blasted in school.

They're all funny.

And pregnant with meaning.

The high school fuck-up who fucks up high schools.

With nothing more than a tweet.

•

He plays a gig on 27 May 2016 AD, this time in West Palm Beach.

Despite this gig getting shut down early, it's the big one.

This is where he reconnects with Geneva Sativa.

•

The *Miami New Times* says that the gig happened in Oakland Park.

But either the location or date is wrong.

By May 2016 AD, there's no way he can play a gig in Florida and not have it generate coverage on YouTube or Twitter.

And there's no evidence anywhere of a gig in Oakland Park.

I'm inclined to think that the date can't be wrong because 27 May 2016 AD is when the deletions of tweets starts hard and fast.

27 MAY 2016 AD: WEST PALM BEACH

And I suspect that this is because the deleted tweets were related, in some way, to Geneva.

*

Before the gig, he comes up and puts his hands around her throat.

She later says she found this sexy.

He invites her to an afterparty.

Within a day, they're living together.

She's with him on-and-off until October 2016 AD.

*

Let me say it again.

Within a day, they're living together.

These are the new children of America.

The spiritual barrenness, the wasted lives in wanton bodies.

This is insanity.

*

By 6 June, "Look At Me!" has nearly 2,000,000 plays.

On 25 June, video emerges of him beating the shit out of someone in a bathroom.

On 27 June, video emerges of him being the shit out of someone else, in a street fight before he plays a gig that night in Orlando.

*

Over the next few months, through until October, he uploads videos of himself and Geneva Sativa.

In some videos, it plays cute.

In others, it plays weird.

The absolute oddest thing that is uploaded, possibly by a minion after he's in lock up, is a video of Geneva undergoing an exorcism.

Or having a drug overdose.

*

During the 27 June fight, when he's rolling around on the ground, he mugs for a photograph.

He's smiling.

His arms are wrapped around the other dude's bloody head.

On 4 July, he uses this photograph as the cover image for a new song that he uploads to SoundCloud.

The song is called "YuNg BrAtZ."

It's a banger.

*

27 JUNE 2016 AD : ORLANDO

On 8 July, he announces that he will release a mixtape called *Bad Vibes Forever.*

On Halloween.

The name is taken from a song by the band Teenage Suicide.

XXX uses it as the name of his record label.

*

But *Bad Vibes Forever* never emerges.

Forthcoming international performances are cancelled.

*

On 14 July 2016 AD, he is arrested for, allegedly, stabbing and robbing one of his former managers.

And thus begins a long season in Hell.

CHAPTER 8

UP ON SENTINEL HILL WITH WILBUR WHATELEY AND YOG-SOTHOTH

By the early months of 2016 AD, it's clear that his music, and his persona have struck a nerve.

*

There's always going to be the easy explanation.

White boys in the suburbs who want venality enacted by a Black boy.

Isn't that the semi-secret official history of hip-hop?

*

To be fair, if you watch YouTube footage of XXXTentacion's live shows, there's a fuckload of White kids in the audience.

But you can also watch YouTube footage of his memorials, including the so-called riot on Melrose Avenue.

The crowds are as mixed as they come.

On 16 December 2015 AD he tweeted: "I make music for weird black kids and agressive white people <3"

*

I don't deny that the entrance point was venality.

It'd be bizarre if it weren't.

Venality is the gateway drug of all pop culture.

But venality is easy as it comes.

Everything in American life is venal.

That isn't what kept them.

*

His rapping was never going to win plaudits from the 50,000 people who care about What Makes a Real MC.

There's no explosion of tight constructions.

Rarely does meaning carry over from one bar to another and change with the next.

The schemes are not especially innovative.

But that's okay.

He wasn't from New York.

And 1994 AD was a long time ago.

*

The telltales are the opening tracks from the two albums that saw commercial release during his lifetime.

17 and *?*.

Their openers are spoken word expositions of each album's respective purpose.

From "The Explanation" on *17*:

> *17*. My collection of nightmares, thoughts, and real life situations I've lived. 17 is the number tattooed on the right side of my head. My own personal number. Soon to be explained in future interviews or instances. By listening to this album, you are literally, and I can not stress this enough, literally entering my mind. And if you are not willing to accept my emotion and hear my words fully, do not listen. I do not value your money. I value your acceptance and loyalty. Here is my pain and thoughts put into words. I put my all into this, in the hopes that it will help cure or at least numb your depression. I love you. Thank you for listening. Enjoy.

Like everything in this book, that blockquote doesn't approach timbre.

The words don't get you near the reality that he sounds different than anything that's come before.

Considering the mic pops, it was probably recorded in his bedroom.

*

"The Explanation" sounds like his tweets.

And that's part of the appeal: he's the first major recording artist without a distinction between his music and an unfiltered social media presence.

*

Rap emerged from a street and party culture.

Being street doesn't lend itself to vulnerability.

No one wants to kick it with the sad person at a party.

(Spoken from personal experience.)

All that showing and proving.

All that swagger.

*

XXXTentacion wasn't immune to masculine posturing or the tonal range that we associate with hip-hop.

That's the challenge of his work.

You have to accept that a totally violent dude can also be defined by questions of self-worth.

You have to accept that someone who could beat the shit out of someone, and use an image of him doing so as the cover image for a song, could also be achingly vulnerable.

*

The way America works is the exact opposite.

Our collective narrative is that you can be one or the other.

You can't be both.

A violent Black man is disallowed the legitimacy of his feelings.

But this is not how people are.

Or how people live.

But it is how their albums are reviewed.

And it's also underlying justification for the entire prison-industrial complex.

*

But what was the nature of that vulnerability?

And why did it travel?

Because be real: in general, nothing is as annoying as hearing another person go on about their suffering.

*

There's more obvious answers, present at the beginning of this book.

The broken home, the missing parents, the criminality, the neglect, the violence, the systemic racism, the inability to love and be loved.

These are the building blocks of another common narrative.

Based on his tweets, I suspect that this common narrative informed XXXTentacion's own sense of self.

*

But I have another theory.

If you had the right eyes and ears, you could look at him, and listen, and know exactly what he was and where he was from.

And I don't mean Broward County.

That dude was from the Internet.

*

There was a world that existed in the same space as our world.

But it was not our world.

Until that world had disappeared, its fundamental definition was unknown to all of its occupants.

And its fundamental definition was this: the old world was the world before merchant bankers discovered the Internet.

It was a world without behaviors constructed by a select group of people making a killing in the financial markets.

It was a world uninformed by the corrupt pseudo-philosophies that informed that select group of people.

It was a world in which human communication had not collapsed into the grotesque exploitation of the species' worst impulses.

*

If you were alive in 1995 AD, it was impossible to look into an LCD screen and watch bukakke anal gangbangs and then, half a second later, look again into that screen and watch someone from Maida Vale behead an American journalist, and then, half a second later, be told by fifty people on social media that you are the living incarnation of evil because you misgendered a character from a fantasy novel.

*

The transformation happened in about twelve years.

It will take centuries to unravel.

If there are centuries.

Another gift of the transformation: the certain knowledge that there is no future.

If it's not global warming, it might be the President on Twitter trolling his way into a nuclear war.

*

Whenever a profound social change occurs, old people always have the same worry.

WHAT ABOUT THE CHILDREN?

Children never ask this question.

And that's because children don't remember any previous life.

*

For children, experience of the moment is always normal.

Imagine XXXTentacion, born in 1998 AD.

He and the Internet grew up together.

They're like the racist ass cracker H.P. Lovecraft's "The Dunwich Horror," in which a young man named Wilbur Whateley is raised alienated from his surrounding society, while his twin brother is a spectral monstrous presence that no one can see and only gets more hideous and dangerous as time passes.

Lovecraft writes Wilbur Whateley as a distinctly unpleasant figure, a bestial presence who works in the service of his grandfather's wicked designs.

But Wilbur Whateley is the story's only sympathetic character.

He was born into a bad situation.

It seems normal that his father is Yog-Sothoth, a whirling ball of primordial malevolent chaos.

And it seems normal that his horrific, invisible brother is kept in a barn.

No one can see the brother.

Everyone knows it's there.

Everyone knows it's getting worse and more monstrous.

Wilbur Whateley keeps on keeping on.

It's all anyone can do.

⋄

XXXTentacion aesthetics are the direct result of the Internet.

He never had a job.

There was a lot of time on house arrest.

And he got kicked out of school.

So what else could he do?

He spent a fuckload of time on YouTube and The Pirate Bay.

⋄

Just because you are born into insanity, and accept it as normal, doesn't make the insanity any less insane.

And human biology is primitive.

People are wired into anxiety.

It's a survival mechanism, the byproduct of evolution, it's what lets you know when you're about to be attacked.

Your body is a machine designed to produce a heightened response to stressful situations.

And every medium, the Internet included, is the extension of that heightened response, and every medium makes a new kind of person.

What happens to the machine when its stressor is the greatest persistent stressor ever faced?

What happens if your interaction with the world is dominated by an engine of human contempt, designed by the ultra-wealthy to inform you that you are less than garbage?

*

After XXXTentacion shaved off his eyebrows in October 2017 AD, he did a long video on Instagram Live.

It's survived on YouTube.

It's remarkable for the intimacy between the artist and his fans.

The vulnerability is off the charts.

No one famous has ever been like this.

*

Someone asks him why he shaved off his eyebrows.

He responds:

> Why no eyebrows? Because I don't want to look like people, I don't want to look everyone else. I wanna be myself and if that means I have to be ugly to look like myself then I'll be ugly. And honestly I'd rather be ugly and attract the real people and attract the real people around me than be, be what everyone wants me to look like and be around a bunch of fake ass niggas that only wanna be around me for some clout. Cause I'm honestly tired of being used. I get used all the time. If you haven't even noticed nigga I don't even wanna be on the fucking Internet as much because of how fucking negative and draining it is.

Other than compassion, the least fashionable idea, circa 2018 AD, is that what doesn't kill you will make you stronger.

We believe the post-9/11 opposite.

How do we keep ourselves safe from old trauma?

The answer has been: hide.

But you can't hide.

Civilization and its false promises are the sheets we drape over old furniture in an abandoned house.

*

For the first eighteen years of his life, XXXTentacion was told— by the world, by the corrections system, by the schools that kicked him out, by the absence of his parents, by the Internet—that he was a piece of shit.

As a result, he had the strength that was weakness.

The violence that revealed the wound.

And my theory is this: to his listeners, his wound mirrored their own wound.

He was the antenna of the moment.

In the eclecticism of person and persona, artist and art, an adolescence brutalized by global capital, the first wank not over a copy of Playboy found in the basement but Skin Diamond in Doctor Whore, sucking a dude off with the help of April O'Neil, a pornstar named after a character from the Teenage Mutant Ninja Turtles, entire lives, with their every stray thought, transformed into the intellectual property of two thousand people from New York, from San Francisco, from Seattle, from Los Angeles, from London, a world of children brutalized by mandatory active shooting training.

RUN. HIDE. FIGHT.

In his wound, and its vastness, if you were someone born into a life where your own purpose was the utility of your flesh to others, you could see what the world had done to you.

CHAPTER 9

BABY IT'S YOU

It falls apart when he stabs his ex-manager.

It's something about money.

The stabbing happens around 5 July 2016 AD.

*

An arrest warrant is issued.

He's picked up on Robbery and Aggravated Battery with a Deadly Weapon.

The details of this crime are obscure.

Tweets have been deleted.

He wasn't yet famous enough to earn the microdetail analysis haunting his latter days.

A few days after the arrest, there's a tweet, apparently, from Geneva on his account: "i love Jahseh - yourl0nelystar"

I'm inclined to say that XXXTentacion authored this tweet himself.

But who knows?

*

While XXXTentacion is in lock-up, which only lasts a few days before he's bonded out, Geneva escapes his apartment.

With the help of some friends.

She moves to Texas.

*

The details of her escape, and his alleged abused of her, are put on Twitter.

The tweets are still there.

They match up with the details that are offered later, when he's arrested for beating her: stompings, drownings, metal objects.

This is the very best evidence that the abuse did happen.

Because it's not coming from anyone who has something to sell.

And it's not coming in the heightened atmosphere of a criminal investigation.

*

I say this without being rude: none of the people involved strike me as individuals who could, over a period of months, keep a false story straight.

*

And these details are being spread, in public.

And lead to nothing.

No criminal investigation.

*

After XXXTentacion bonds out, he's quiet for a few days.

And then he's arrested again on 9 August 2016 AD.

This time it's Aggravated Battery and Home Assault.

This time it's for that shit back in November 2015 AD.

The robbery where he stole some technology and pistol whipped a guy.

The robbery where his victim identifies him from a photograph on Twitter.

*

It's been less than a year but that time was packed with more life than most people experience in a decade.

He's making money from his music, from selling shirts and merch, from touring.

He's been fucking witches and attending exorcisms.

He is known anywhere that people roll with underground hip-hop.

He's become one of the most famous performers in Florida.

But now the past has come calling.

*

Maybe Jahseh Onfroy is dead.

But that's still the name on the arrest sheet.

*

He's stuck in jail until 19 September 2016 AD.

He gets out on bond.

Geneva's back from Texas.

She moves in with him.

Don't judge.

They live in Sweetwater.

*

And then it gets even worse.

*

On 8 October 2016 AD, XXXTentacion is arrested for Kidnapping/False Imprisonment and Aggravated Battery on a Pregnant Victim.

CHAPTER 10

GENEVA

There are several ways to Google for Geneva.

If you search on her Internet aliases, the multinational megacorporation will return, in its first five results, a subreddit dedicated to sharing her homemade pornography.

You can watch her fuck, you can watch her dildo up, you can watch her suck dick.

If you Google her real name, you can find reality consensus being made.

Even before XXXTentacion's death, the media had descended on Geneva.

Before I go any further.

Some days its feels like I'm the last person in America who believes in the presumption of innocence before guilt.

Especially when it comes to accused Black men.

And XXXTentacion is too dead to ever have a trial.

But somebody beat that girl.

Given that he will have no trial, I don't think there's anything wrong in saying that I find it more than likely than XXXTentacion was the responsible party.

But that's based on conjecture.

No evidence was actually presented.

The only thing I can do is go with the information I have.

And for a very long time, my information was based on *Pitchfork* running a 1592 word summary of a 142-page deposition transcript.

And if a 1592 word article on *Pitchfork* is how we now establish total guilt and social excommunication, then it's time to refresh the tree of liberty with the blood of patriots & tyrants.

*

But then I saw those tweets from July 2016 AD.

And I knew.

Somebody beat that girl.

And it was him.

*

Several months into #MeToo, the website *Quillette* ran an interview with Samantha Geimer.

Samantha Geimer's long journey in consensus reality goes back to 1977 AD, when she was raped by the film director Roman Polanski, who was forty-four years old.

She was thirteen years old.

She's been dealing with this shit for forty-one years.

Whatever you think about Quilette, Samantha Geimer's spent her whole adult life living at the intersection of abuse, celebrity and media.

She's the OG of #MeToo.

In the interview, she says this:

> Why are women so astute at judging when a man has used them sexually, but apparently oblivious to how those in the media use them that is, in its own way, just as wrong?

*

Whenever I think about Geneva, what I feel is a great pity.

It's obvious that her relationship with XXXTentacion will be the most important thing in her life.

She will be haunted until she changes her name.

And even then.

*

If I were creating consensus reality, I'd argue that XXXTentacion should be blamed for Geneva's life being ruined.

But then I'd be doing the same thing as everyone else who manufactures morality.

I'd be lying.

*

Even before the beating, Geneva was in the new social dynamic.

And no one alive, let alone someone in their early twenties, can comprehend its contours and implications.

*

Here's how life used to work: you could be young, and you could exist, and you could do stupid fucking shit, and unless you'd been caught up in the criminal justice system, you could walk away from that stupid shit.

And while that stupid fucking shit might cause difficulty in transitioning into another life, you could escape it.

But now every minutia of detail is monetizable content.

Almost nothing goes away, and people make money for their masters, and every shred of information is used to enrich a transnational class of about 100,000 people.

This isn't even about Geneva or XXXTentacion.

This is about you, reader.

Your life is the property of others.

There is no longer any need for vast apparatuses of state security and secret police.

Every stupid thing that you do, in public or in private, is recorded by someone's smartphone.

And they're going to snitch.

And the world will know.

And the people who rule the world will make serious money off your transgression.

Every pussy is up for grabs.

Good luck with the future.

*

Think about Geneva.

Her early life was shitty.

It didn't give her the best judgment.

She moved in with a dude in May 2016 AD.

He was a local musician with a rabid online fanbase.

Honestly, the fame's probably an initial turn-on.

It always is.

They were together for about four months.

Whatever else, they were in love.

And don't romanticize that point.

Don't Sid & Nancy that shit up.

Being in love is fucking common.

It's an easy emotion.

Anyone can be in love for four months.

During their time together, his fame expanded, a little, and his notoriety expanded, a little, but he wasn't yet megamedia explosive.

She is abused several times, culminating in the beating that causes his arrest.

And that final beating is awful.

Her skull gets cracked.

Her eyeball gets fucked up.

He refuses to let her get medical attention.

She escapes from his house while he's playing *Minecraft*.

With his fans.

She posts a photo on Twitter.

She looks like warmed over death.

It's awful.

And because he's got a rabid fanbase, and because his whole life has been documented for the sake of our economic masters, when he's arrested, everyone all ready knows the name of his girlfriend.

She's been in videos that he's uploaded.

And now he's in jail.

And she's being talked about on Twitter, on Reddit, on Snapchat, on Instagram.

And then, a few months later, while still in jail, he is catapulted into true fame.

And then he's on the *Hot 100.*

And in the middle of his ascent, *Pitchfork* reports on her deposition.

Pitchfork doesn't name her.

But it doesn't matter.

It's all over the Internet.

And the outro track on *17* is titled with her last name.

And then the media is everywhere.

And she's making pornography on the Internet, trying to cop a couple of bucks from Onlyfriends.

And then it just keeps going.

And then he's dead, and she's going to his memorial and getting into fights with his fans.

*

There'll always be diehards who suggest that she deserves whatever she gets.

But that's wrong.

No one alive deserves the beatings, or the subsequent media coverage, because she dated someone in 2016 AD.

*

It's the Wilbur Whateley thing again.

An entire generation of kids raised to believe that their exploitation is a normal way of life.

And don't make any mistake: the whole thing is class coded.

Rich kids don't suffer the same Internet as poor kids.

Just watch Twitch or homemade pornography.

You can tell by the home furnishings that the content is created by the working classes.

Or, in rare cases, the nouveau riche.

*

XXXTentacion and Geneva must be the first instance, in the history of the world, where a person accused of battering someone, and their accuser, have multiple online videos of them fucking other people.

And none of the participants are pornographic professionals.

*

Maybe I've got the wrong impression.

Maybe she has a happy life and thinks that her interface with the mechanics of fame have worked out well.

If that's the case, then I'm full of shit.

But I keep thinking about Samantha Geimer.

*

You can tell that Geneva was not a person born into a situation with much hope.

She had an absent mother, a father with thirteen other kids, she hopped around homes, her mom kicked her out.

And this was all before she was sixteen.

*

The idea that anyone can do anything in America is bullshit.

Most people aren't born with the natural gifts, or experience the random luck, that will allow them to transcend their social class.

And most people don't have parents who can afford an education that allows their ungifted children to transcend.

*

I know what I'm talking about.

No one has transcended their social origins more than me.

I'm a suckcess story.

I came from a single-parent household in Buttfuck Nowhere and, through sheer force of will, transformed myself into the last real American dissident intellectual.

You'll never see the like again!

*

I fucked up public school so badly that I had no hope of graduating.

In my case, the fucking up didn't matter.

I was born with a natural gift.

I'm smart as the dickens.

And I had the financial means to go to private school.

My private school offered an alternative education.

I had what XXXTentacion begged for in 2013 AD.

And never received.

*

There were a ton of kids in my public school who weren't smart as the dickens.

They were dumb as doorknobs.

They were also fucking up.

And they ended up with lives indistinguishable from the lives of their parents.

The only difference between their lives and their parents' lives is that the collapse of the American prosperity bubble meant the kids from my high school had less chances for economic advancement than their mommas and poppas.

*

Here's how much I've transcended my social origins: a few months ago, on the strength of having published several obscene books about gay sex and the Internet, I was asked by my private high school to be the Guest of Honor at their annual fundraiser.

I was the Successful Alumnus who returned like a conquering hero.

I gave a speech to a room full of rich people.

And because I am sort-of writer famous, and because I am good at public speaking, the rich people hung on my every word.

I murdered that crowd by reiterating the central illusion of America life and soothing their consciences about their relative place in the hierarchy of global evil.

I pretended that anything was possible for anyone if they were given enough opportunity.

•

But most people are like Geneva.

They're the people described by Henry David Thoreau:

> The mass of men serve the State thus, not as men mainly, but as machines, with their bodies. They are the standing army, and the militia, gaolers, constables, posse comitatus, etc. In most cases there is no free exercise whatever of the judgment or of the moral sense; but they put themselves on a level with wood and earth and stones; and wooden men can perhaps be manufactured that will serve the purpose as well.

If nothing else, this quote proves that Thoreau was a total dick.

He's blaming working class people for being working class, rather than acknowledging that the state creates the conditions in which most people can only serve with their bodies.

Thoreau might be a dick, but that doesn't mean he's wrong.

Most people can only serve the state, which is now indistinguishable from the financial class that operates the Internet, with their bodies.

Which is what Geneva has done.

And that's putting aside the amateur porn.

Her physical presence—the detailed reports on her injuries and her photos and videos—has made an unquantifiable amount of money for the people manufacturing morality about her victimization.

That's a horrible thing to have happen when you're twenty-two.

It's like a curse on an Egyptian tomb.

It's going to follow her until the day she dies.

And it's an awful price to pay when you didn't do anything outside the range of normal human behavior.

*

If I had to give advice to anyone under the age of thirty, it would be the exact opposite of what I told that room full of rich people.

I am a man who, through sheer force of will and cunning, penetrated to the other side when absolutely no one wanted me.

I've been on television, I've been on radio, I've been written about (favorably but not for long) by *The New York Times*, by *The Washington Post*, by *The Wall Street Journal*, by *The Guardian*, and ten thousand other outlets of the worldwide metropolitan liberal elite.

I am a bestselling author in multiple countries.

And I achieved this on the strength of a self-published book.

Having enacted my needless exercise in proving a point, I learned the truth of what I had always suspected.

There is no reward in human achievement.

Status, power, fame, cash.

It's all shit.

In a post-industrialized economy, the only thing that money is good for, really, is the down payment on an ugly home.

And better legal representation.

*

Here is my advice.

If the whole game is rigged, and your behavior is constructed by invisible social pressures, then there's only one thing you can do.

Do every thing wrong!

*

Everyone knows that there's a right way to behave.

If you want a career in the arts, you've got to pay your dues before you pay the rent.

But when you get to the other side—when you're an actual suckcess—what you discover is that the rules only function as gears in a machine that constructs another kind of wooden man.

You can do every thing right.

You can pay your dues.

But you'd better never ask who's collecting.

And you'd better never look in the mirror.

*

But if you do every thing wrong?

*

It's something that XXXTentacion understood on an implicit level, although I don't think he understood it well enough to distinguish between doing things wrong and, on occasion, being an asshole.

Wrong means a successful career driven by all the things that people tell you will kill your career.

Wrong gets you on the *Billboard* charts with some shit you uploaded to SoundCloud.

Or bestseller lists with a book that you published from beneath your bed.

Being an asshole means dooming a twenty-two year old woman to a lifetime of media exploitation.

Or breaking the heart of your long term girlfriend because you can't deal with the pressures of being interviewed by Germans about the Internet.

*

To her credit, Geneva understands media victimization.

A day after XXXTentacion died, she sent out two tweets.

Tweet #1: "i know y'all don't fuck w me, but this isn't about me. just please stop tagging me in disrespectful threads and arguments. i honestly don't care for any of the hype. i lost someone close to me. leave me alone."

Tweet #2: "it's disgusting that people are speaking for me. i don't care if no one cared about me however many months ago, i didn't lose my life. he did. it's permanent. i'm still here. like how do you think that makes me feel? everyone expecting me to be relieved or happy?! no, i'm broken."

*

And I'm no different than the people I'm criticizing.

I'm another vulture writing about someone who doesn't deserve the scrutiny.

This book is, by its nature, a further victimization.

*

Eventually the bruises go away.

The broken bones heal.

But print is forever.

*

So I'll do something that no one ever does.

I'll apologize without anyone asking for the apology.

*

Geneva.

I'm sorry.

And not just for this chapter.

For life.

You didn't deserve any of it.

CHAPTER 11

I'D LIKE TO BE ROTTED OUT JUST BEFORE I BCUM AWARE OF THE PAIN

He spends months in jail.

Fall going into Winter.

Not much happens.

Audio of him phoning from prison circulates on Twitter.

*

In early 2017 AD, Drake previews a song called "KMT."

It's a bad cover version of "Look at Me!"

*

When it comes to shitty radio, Drake is the lowest of the low.

He's from Canada, he used to act on *Degrassi*, and he's mastered a fluency with hip-hop culture while coming across as a relatable middle class brother.

This is the message of Drake's public persona: *He won't steal your PSP. But watch out! He's still unpredictable! He might bring your girl flowers!*

He's the darling of the Righteous Whites who write about hip-hop, and he's dominated for a decade.

If there's an obvious ideological enemy, then it's Drake.

*

"KMT" spurs a social media beef with Drake, taken up not only by XXXTentacion but also his fans.

Shortly thereafter, "Look At Me!" gets commercial release.

Its cover art is the mugshot taken after his arrest in October 2016 AD.

It's an instant icon, one the greatest American photographs from the last few decades.

Aattach it to anything and you'll make money.

Which is why it's the banner illustration for fathomless articles of manufactured morality.

Everyone wants to cash in.

The photograph looks like this:

"Look At Me!" is now on paid streaming platforms.

Combine that and the mugshot and the fact that the song has been gaining steam for over a year, and XXXTentacion ends up on the *Billboard Hot 100.*

While he's still in jail.

*

Now he's rent the veil.

He's hot on the charts.

Success is morality.

And he's a big time sinner.

*

In April 2017 AD, XXXTentacion is released from jail.

The second day out, he tweets that Drake's mom can catch a dick.

*

In May, XXXTentacion flies in a sixteen year old girl from Ohio.

Her name is Jocelyn Flores.

She's supposed to do some modeling.

Or maybe it's romantic.

Some money disappears from his house.

She squabbles with another girl, which freaks out XXXTentacion because he's got so much heat.

He sends her to a hotel room.

She kills herself.

*

In June, XXXTentacion and $ki Mask the Slump God go out on The Revenge Tour.

The tour takes its name from the *Revenge* mixtape, which he releases in May 2017 AD.

It's his first album-length commercial release.

It's the best of the old SoundCloud stuff.

*

The tour is a glorious disaster.

Videos emerge of XXXTentacion fighting fans, XXXTentacion getting knocked out on stage, XXXTentacion's handlers accidentally throwing him into a crowd barricade.

*

While he's on the road, *XXL* magazine releases its 2017 AD Freshman Class issue.

XXL's Freshman Class is an annual list of up-and-coming rappers.

It's a perennial editorial stunt designed to move issues in the dead summer months.

Nine of the 2017 AD Freshman Class are chosen by the magazine's editors.

The tenth is chosen by online poll.

XXXTentacion dominates the voting.

*

The tour is scheduled for twenty-six dates.

XXXTentacion manages eleven shows before he postpones the rest, although he does play the final date in Florida.

He cites mental and physical health issues.

*

XXL releases video of a Freshman Class cypher with four of the chosen: Playboi Carti, Madeintyo, Ugly God, and XXXTentacion.

*

The other three use the cypher to rap about what hip-hop's been mired in since Diddy murdered the Golden Age.

Diamonds, thots, that purp, stripclubs, Louis Vuitton, cash, insults to unnamed foes, probably something about cars.

After standing in shadow at the back of the room, haunting the proceedings like a spectre, XXXTentacion performs last.

His verse is delivered a capella while he's crouched on the floor.

It's about—I think—a murderous fantasy of the apocalypse, the hypocrisy of Christians who bow before the scandalous clergy, the devil being part of human nature, plotting a murder, being the son of a demon, and the impossibility of knowing the rewards of faith before death.

It's thirty-seven seconds long.

It steals the show.

And if the above description sounds like horrorcore, please know that it isn't.

It's new, there's never been anything like it, and you can't remember anything that came before.

*

The rest of 2017 AD is a depressing slog of fame.

The highpoints are the August release of *17*, his first real album, and *A Ghetto Christmas Carol* in December.

They demonstrate how far his music has come.

And how quickly.

They're a million miles from *Revenge*.

No one sounds like this.

He's gone from being a SoundCloud kid to the most consequential recording artist of the last decade.

And it happened in less than a year.

*

17 enters the *Billboard Top 200* at #2.

But then there's the Jahseh Onfrony luck: every time something good happens, it's followed by something terrible.

Two weeks after *17* drops, *Pitchfork* publishes a summary of Geneva's pre-trial deposition.

It's not much of an exclusive.

Don't forget: all of this shit has been on Twitter.

And no one noticed or cared until he started making real money.

*

On 30 October, I email him about blurbing a book that I'm publishing.

It's an old address, but I hope it works.

He never responds.

*

He gets arrested a few days after the release of *A Ghetto Christmas Carol.*

The charges are multiple counts of witness tampering and come after his defense introduces an affidavit, signed by Geneva, in which she says she no longer wants him prosecuted.

The witness tampering charges derive from the period when he was sitting in jail and making phone calls from inside.

He's come full circle.

It's like @fuckjahseh has returned.

*

After he's dead, the calls and audio of him from just before the October 2016 AD arrest are released.

The prison calls are the product of mental illness.

There's no other way to describe someone who spends 16 hours on the phone in a 46 hour period.

It's someone have an episode.

He's being warned at the beginning of every call that it's being recorded and that anything he says can be used against him, and he's still confessing to a wide range of criminality.

Including, arguably, beating Geneva.

*

If you believe the Righteous Whites, the recordings complicate his legacy.

Here's how it's all reported: *XXXTentacion's Confession of Domestic Abuse!*

But the calls and secret recording are weird, because it feels like he's back in that *No Jumper*/thug life lying.

Example: he talks about the January 2016 AD stabbing incident.

He says that he stabbed ten people.

As can best be established, this isn't true.

He only stabbed three or four.

Which ain't great.

But it's that exaggeration shit again.

And, true to form for reporting by Righteous Whites, the one thing that the tapes do not contain is an unambiguous confession of beating Geneva.

*

After the December 2017 AD arrest, he enters 2018 AD facing twenty charges in total.

Here's an accidental reflection of America: the witness tampering charges are more serious than the charges of beating and kidnapping Geneva.

They carry a stiffer sentence.

If he gets convicted on everything, he'll go to prison for decades.

*

But that would never happen.

The witness tampering charges are how American prosecution works.

The alleged criminal is charged with as many things as possible.

This lowers the likelihood of the accused being found innocent at trial and threatens them with decades locked in a room.

You charge someone with fifteen counts of witness tampering because you want them to plead out to a smaller number of charges.

Wrack up a win and avoid the hassle of trial.

*

2018 AD is the end.

He starts the year in a very familiar place: on house arrest.

Until he gets shot, things are unusually quiet.

*

His second album *?* is released in March 2018 AD by Caroline Distribution, which is part of Capitol Records, which is part of Universal Music Group, which is owned by the French conglomerate Vivendi.

Now he's working for the same people as everyone else.

According to news reports, he did a one-album deal for $6,000,000.

Don't believe that.

The numbers attached to entertainment deals are always inflated.

And, by this point, he's big enough that even if he did make a deal for $6,000,000, there's an army of managers, agents and lawyers.

Whose cut will be paid before taxes.

*

The lead single off *?* is "SAD!"

What can be said?

It's another fucking monster.

*

Every time something good happens.

A week after the album's release, debuting at #1 on the *Hot 200*, an old SnapChat video leaks.

In which he apparently punches a woman in the head.

Of all the violence that's accrued to him, to my eyes this one is the most unclear.

It looks staged and there's no sound.

The whole thing ends up with XXXTentacion suing the woman in the video.

*

About a month before he dies, Spotify decides that it can no longer promote purveyors of quote-Hateful Content-unquote on its editorial and algorithmically curated playlists.

Spotify was funded by Silicon Valley.

It's unprofitable.

The new policy defines Hateful Content as "content that expressly and principally promotes, advocates, or incites hatred or violence against a group or individual based on characteristics, including, race, religion, gender identity, sex, ethnicity, nationality, sexual orientation, veteran status, or disability."

It's difficult to verify, but it appears that the only two artists affected are R. Kelly and XXXTentacion, neither of who ever released a song which would get them shamed and named by the Southern Poverty Law Center.

Because the new policy is a bullshit PR move, Spotify doesn't even consider removing "Sweet Home Alabama."

Despite decades of denials from Lynyrd Skynyd, "Sweet Home Alabama" is a song that is explicit in its support of segregation.

It's literally a cracker carol about Governor George Wallace defying the Supreme Court's 1954 AD landmark decision in Brown -v- the Board of Education.

Draw your own conclusions.

*

And then it's over.

On 18 June 2018 AD, driving his car, XXXTentacion gets shot in the neck.

He's outside of a motorcycle dealership.

He's twenty years old.

A hot minute after he dies, people upload videos of XXXTentacion dead in his car.

The video quality is super shitty.

Pixelated messes shot by people who don't know how to turn their smartphones to a horizontal orientation.

On Twitter, some people pray that he's still alive.

But if you've ever watched something die, you can recognize the stillness.

You know.

The ghost had been given.

That night, I make a tasteless joke to a friend: "He died like he lived."

"What do you mean?" asks the friend.

"He died like he lived," I said. "In a shitty video on the Internet."

*

A week after his death, "SAD!" hits #1 on the *Hot 100.*

CHAPTER 12

RIDE AND DIE

On 8 October 2016 AD, XXXTentacion was arrested for allegedly beating Geneva.

This was a day after the Washington Post published video of Donald J. Trump talking about grabbing pussy.

*

The pussy tape really resonated with people.

I honestly don't know why.

*

I'm not an idiot.

*

Of course I know why.

*

By the time of Donald J. Trump's impossible victory, the Presidency had transformed into an office dedicated to blowing up illiterate Muslim peasants with radio controlled airplanes.

What I honestly do not know is why we place a premium on the apparent personal dignity of human beings elected to an office where they will wage war against half the world.

But that's the old American hypocrisy.

Whenever we hire someone to murder Brown, Black and Asian people, they'd better have beautiful table manners.

*

After Trump won the election in 2016 AD, the Liberals of America faced a total collapse of their political agenda.

They were hella out of power.

The only place left to exert their agency was over arts and culture.

This always happens after a massive political failure.

*

The refocusing on the American arts meant that a reckoning was coming.

Alas, XXXTentacion was made for this moment.

He had done everything wrong: he was Black, he was young, he was too honest on the Internet, he'd bragged about beating up a gay kid, and he'd been accused of beating the shit out of his pregnant ex-girlfriend.

And worse than anything: he was successful.

Kids really loved his music.

And him.

And they gave neither a fuck nor a tuppence about morality manufactured by Righteous Whites living in Brooklyn and Chicago.

*

This is because the business models of the Internet, which were clickbait disguised as virtue, had produced a massive disconnect between the people who make media, and write about it, and the people who consume media.

It's easiest to see this with television.

Every year, the commentariat favor at least one new television series.

They will write ten thousand articles and a billion thinkpieces about this series.

But when you see the ratings on these series—something now sort-of possible with streaming originals—you realize that almost no one is watching them.

Girls.

Twin Peaks: The Return.

Transparent.

And yeah, network executives always give bullshit excuse about time-shifted viewing and an online audience.

But when you're playing defense from the start, there's an obvious truth.

No one cares.

Success is the only determinant of morality in America.

But morality in America was undergoing a serious reexamination.

And in that reevaluation, XXXTentacion represented an inherent contradiction.

If there was a general consensus amongst the commentariat that success was good, and only Good People could be successful, and the creation of art was the domain of people who were Good, then how could a person who'd done every thing wrong also be successful?

And his success wasn't like *Girls.*

His cultural prominence was not a diadem crown of manufactured morality.

His work wasn't a chamber piece for the select and knowing few.

He did it the hard way.

The real way.

Through a groundswell of actual support from a mass of people.

Which made it undeniable.

In 1947 AD, the French lunatic Antonin Artaud published *Van Gogh, le suicidé de la société.*

Artaud's theory is that Van Gogh did not commit suicide but rather that society, through a collective consciousness of hate, tortured Van Gogh.

The suicide was the product of this torture.

Or something like that.

I haven't read Artaud in about twenty years.

I may be misremembering the whole thing.

I also believe that Artaud posits the collective consciousness attacks at night.

All the normal people project their loathing.

The loathing arrives as nightmares in the head of the sleeping individual.

*

Back in 1947 AD, this idea must have been fanciful.

Now it just sounds like the Internet.

Remember that Instagram Live video:

> Why no eyebrows? Because I don't want to look like people, I don't want to look everyone else. I wanna be myself and if that means I have to be ugly to look like myself then I'll be ugly. And honestly I'd rather be ugly and attract the real people and attract the real people around me than be, be what everyone wants me to look like and be around a bunch of fake ass niggas that only wanna be around me for some clout. Cause I'm honestly tired of being used. I get used all the time. If you haven't even noticed nigga I don't even wanna be on the fucking Internet as much because of how fucking negative and draining it is.

*

He'd been raised on, and by, the Internet.

His entire career was the Internet.

And it'd come to that.

*

The crazy ass dude who fights people, who lives in borderline poverty, who says whatever the hell he wants on Twitter.

When he's fourteen.

When he's out hitting licks.

When he's the lowest of the low.

It's an approach to life.

But you can't be that person when everyone is watching.

You can't live that wild, in public, without the collective consciousness figuring out a way to suicide you.

•

The total dominance of Black people in American pop culture—something that, as recently as twenty-five years ago, was unimaginable—means that all of the Righteous Whites who create consensus reality around media are also people who grew up listening to hip-hop and Black music.

It creates a push-and-pull that plays on out racial lines.

The Righteous Whites who create consensus reality can easily say positive things about crap like Drake or Migos.

No one cares, no one notices.

But criticizing Black artists puts them into a difficult position.

If anything is kryptonite to Righteous Whites, it's not being racially prejudiced, which they are, but the thought that someone, somewhere might call them racist.

They might get fired!

David Remnick might blush!

*

One of the secret goals of the people who create consensus reality is to find Black people whose transgressions are so severe that they are open to criticism without anyone being called racist.

And even if you do get called racist for this criticism, it won't matter.

Usually it's just dudes on Twitter who are into melanin theology and defending Bill Cosby.

People who can be safely ignored.

*

The whole thing is a variation on a quest perilous.

And as I wrote much earlier in this book, this is the nature of that quest: to find another O.J. Simpson.

*

Spotify's Hateful Content policy zeroed in on R. Kelly and XXXTentacion.

You can see why.

Everyone in America watched R. Kelly pissing all over a teenager.

He was marked out as a Bad Man.

And XXXTentacion was always doing something stupid on the Internet, and he was an avant-gardist, which meant that there wasn't hardened Black opinion around his work, and there was that *Pitchfork* exposé of Geneva's deposition against him, leaked after Donald J. Trump's pussy tape created a national reckoning on the treatment of women amongst the people who manufacture consensus reality.

And its legalese slotted him into O.J. territory.

And he'd bragged about beating up a gay kid.

*

For a while, Chris Brown was part of this elite clique.

He seems to have gotten out.

Probably because of misogynoir.

*

If the people who manufacture consensus reality had any power, or their opinions mattered to anyone who didn't work in media or politics, then the career of XXXTentacion would have been impossible.

The millions of words produced on deadline for money would have been a hard stop on his ambitions.

There is the world as it is represented.

And then there is the world as it lived.

Nothing frustrates people more than learning the extent of their own uselessness.

His death provoked the usual.

A user comment on *Jezebel* distills it down:

> I can't say that I am sorry this abusive, terrifying and completely evil man can't hurt anyone ever again. In fact, I needed some good news yesterday. This fit the bill.

As does another:

> I think that it can be better for society overall if some people die (I'm not advocating murder, but if they fall off a cliff I won't be shedding any tears). I don't know much about his life but, sometimes, people just come out wrong or don't add any value to society (exponentially, stupendously worse but Ted Bundy comes to mind - something was just wrong with him from the get-go. God made a mistake).

In 2004 AD, Irene V. Blair, Charles M. Judd and Kristine M. Chapleau published an article in the journal *Psychological Science.*

The article was titled "The Influence of Afrocentric Facial Features in Criminal Sentencing."

Building on their past research, the article recounts an experiment.

Photographs of 216 people were split into groups of White and Black people.

These photographs where then shown to volunteers in a study.

The volunteers were asked to determine who had the most Afrocentric features.

Afrocentric was defined as: dark skin, wide nose, coarse hair, full lips.

In other words, this:

All the photographs were mugshots.

Like the photo above, they'd been taken by the Florida Department of Corrections.

*

The authors' previous studies had shown that people, in general, were very good at judging who had Afrocentric features.

That wasn't the point of the 2004 AD study.

The idea to take the photographs of convicted criminals, and then ask people to determine who amongst the convicted had Afrocentric features, and then see if the presence of Afrocentric features had any relationship to the length of a convict's criminal sentence.

The authors found that, when it came to the convicts who possessed Afrocentric features, they pulled longer sentences.

The authors further found that this correlation was statistically more significant than race or previous criminal history.

Neither of these two factors were particularly predictive of a criminal sentence.

They also found that the Afrocentric correlation cut across races.

White people determined to have Afrocentric features also pulled longer sentences.

The White people with Afrocentric features actually pulled longer sentences than Black people with Afrocentric features.

*

In 2016 AD, the people who manufacture consensus reality destroyed the career of Nate Parker.

He was a Black man who'd been found not guilty of rape by a White jury in rural Pennsylvania.

Fifteen years earlier.

How the hell do you flood the Internet with vacuous statements about neoliberal political theater and then throw a dude overboard when he's managed to achieve the one thing that you've spent years claiming was impossible?

If you've spent three years cramming support for Black Lives Matter between your tweets about hot yoga and vaping legal weed, then I think you have an obligation to not roll over like a dog waiting for a stomach scratch whenever a Black dude you don't like is caught up in the criminal justice system.

*

And that's not the only hypocrisy, is it?

*

Consensus reality is manufactured on devices that are embodiments of global evil.

Look at your smartphone: it's filled with minerals strip mined by child slaves in the Congo.

The mineral profits fund wars.

And you never hear about those wars.

They happen in a part of the world that no one cares about.

*

The minerals then get sent to China, where other slaves put them in phones and computers.

And these devices are used to manufacture consensus reality.

There is literally no way to have an opinion, in public, in 2018 AD, and not be involved in the hierarchy of global evil.

This book is a good example.

Despite its intentions, this is a byproduct of global evil.

*

Most of the people writing those articles were residents in a country that'd made a cottage industry out wreaking havoc on the rest of the world.

*

The Watson Institute at Brown University has a project called The Costs of War.

In early 2018 AD, they released a map of locations in the United States Counterterror War.

It involved 76 countries.

That's 39% of the countries on Earth.

Twenty of them are in sub-Saharan Africa.

*

This was how morality was manufactured.

This was how consensus reality around media was created.

By people who lived in the world's greatest war machine.

By people whose taxes paid for secret wars in sub-Saharan Africa and radio controlled airplanes that dropped bombs on villages of Muslims peasants.

By people who wrote their morality on devices built with slave labor.

By the people who had ethnically cleansed the Fillmore, Bed-Stuy, and Dogtown, and then tweeted about Black Lives Matters.

And by people who, faced with all of the above, believed the worst thing that could happen was a sketchy dude from Florida ending up on the *Billboard Top 100.*

*

Given *Jezebel*'s target audience, I can't imagine those two comments being made by anyone other than a pair of good liberals.

And I can't imagine why they bothered to write full sentences.

Honestly, they should have just spared everyone the bother.

In the words of Carl Stokes: they should've just called him a nigger.

#Resist.

*

XXXTentacion was Bad.

And success is Good.

And a Bad person should not be allowed to partake of the Good.

Remember the title of that *Pitchfork* article.

"XXXTentacion is Blowing Up Behind Bars. Should He Be?"

*

There's an old rule in journalism.

If a headline arrives in the form of a yes/no question, then the answer is always no.

*

I thought about including quotes from some of the more scabrous things people wrote about XXXTentacion.

But I decided against it.

I'm sick of a culture built around naming and shaming.

And I believe in forgiveness.

*

It has occurred to me that XXXTentacion functions as an easy way for members of the commentariat to signal their own virtue.

If you want to up the Righteousness, all you need do is mention his litany of sins.

Bashing him is an easy rhetorical device.

It stakes out your position.

It shows the world What You Believe.

When confronted with these statements of belief, I always wonder: *is this being done for money or is this being done to hide the sins of the self?*

Because other than earning cash dollars off Geneva's beatings, the only reason for writing a negative posthumous article about XXXTentacion is for the writer of said article to make the world aware that they are a Good Person.

And who the fuck needs to do that?

Only people haunted by their own past.

Who are establishing a backcatalogue of righteousness as a counterbalance for when the reckoning arrives.

*

If XXXTentacion shouldn't have been blowing up behind bars, then, what, exactly should he have been doing?

His upbringing was marked by a lack of formal education or any hope of economic advancement.

Before he started uploading music to SoundCloud, he had only one possible future.

Serving the state with his body.

The belief that he should have no reward in life contains its own unasked and unanswered question: what measurable social good could have come from XXXTentacion not having a successful career?

⋄

The unspoken implication is what bothers me the most.

All the criticism, all the music writing, all the morality manufactured for money on deadline by people using devices built by slaves.

This is what they were saying: *Jahseh Onfroy, from nothing you have come and to nothing we will return you.*

⋄

If we had to think about every incident of violence, and its causes, and the mental state of the person who committed that crime, we couldn't function as a society.

America has so internalized the logic of the prison state that this logic has become the de facto justification of our civilization.

But there's a pathology in the constructed behaviors of our society.

On 6 March 2014 AD, XXXTentacion tweets: "so fucking happy , my dad called me , asked me to rap for all his homies on the cell block , and them niggas freaked out"

And follows it up with: "nigga told me he was proud of me"

This pathology can't excuse individual behaviors or choices.

But, Jesus Christ, can it ever explain them.

*

Call me sentimental, but I don't believe that XXXTentacion was defined by his worst actions.

I'm not even sure that a person's worst actions mean anything.

I don't think that fucking up when you're young means that a person should be banished from our society.

Especially when the people who've fucked up aren't from bastions of privilege and power.

Particularly when, like XXXTentacion, they are people in need and people who ask, repeatedly, for help in experiencing personal change.

I don't see any good in prison.

And I don't see any good in his death.

*

And this isn't an argument I'm making because XXXTentacion had natural gifts that allowed him to transcend his social class.

I find this true of almost everyone.

*

But he lived too free, too wild, and too open.

And the collective consciousness took note.

The only possible sentence was death.

*

The nature of his demise was a reminder of where he'd come from.

That dude got jacked.

White rappers don't die from a bullet in the neck.

They OD.

White rappers can turn off the theatrics.

They've got parents who went to Harvard.

In the end, they're tourists.

*

In a way, XXXTentacion too was a tourist.

It's the paradox of his life.

He was the poor Black rapper who most wanted the life of a nerdy White boy at a time when what nerdy White boys wanted most was the lives of poor Black rappers.

And no one, especially he himself, would let him live the life that he wanted.

*

But the vacation always ends.

You always have to go back home.

*

But I've only got one thing to say to the kids who, despite the endless articles, fucked with XXXTentacion.

Good for you.

You were right.

Printed in Great Britain
by Amazon

55401467R00106